203 PAPER PIECING Patterns

ABOUT THE PAPER PIECING & PAGE DESIGNERS:

TODDI BARCLAY   **SHAUNA BERGLUND-IMMEL**   **PARIS DUKES**   **LENAE GERIG**   **ARLENE PETERSON**

Toddi Barclay is the newest member of the Hot Off The Press design team. She is a Scrapbook Specialist and collage fanatic. She lives in Washington with her husband, Brian, and their dog, Pete.

Shauna Berglund-Immel is a Scrapbook Specialist that loves lumpy pages. Shauna lives in Oregon with her husband, Dave, and their two children, Spencer and Kaelin.

Paris Dukes is a Scrapbook Specialist and especially loves paper piecing. Paris lives in Oregon with her husband, Jim, and their daughter, Natalie.

LeNae Gerig is a Scrapbook Specialist and our in-house craft expert. She lives in Oregon with her husband, Chris, their daughter, Lauren, and their dog, Bailey.

Arlene Peterson is a Scrapbook Specialist and teaches scrapbooking classes across the United States. She lives in Oregon with her huband, Craig, their youngest daughter, Missy, and their two dogs, Kookie and Nike.

ABOUT THE ARTISTS:

Annie Lang is a self-taught artist who works from her home studio in Michigan. She relies on her husband and three sons to provide inspiration for her whimsical characters.

Jacie Pete is a Graphic Artist for the Hot Off The Press design team. She has over 20 years of experience as an illustrator and art teacher.

Joy Schaber is also a Graphic Artist for the Hot Off The Press design team. She has a degree in Animation from the Art Institute of Seattle.

PRODUCTION CREDITS:
- **President:** Paulette Jarvey
- **Vice-President:** Teresa Nelson
- **Production Manager:** Lynda Hill
- **Editors:** Paulette Jarvey, Lynda Hill
- **Project Editor:** India de Kanter
- **Photographer:** John McNally
- **Graphic Designers:** Jacie Pete, Joy Schaber
- **Digital Imagers:** Victoria Weber, Scott Gordon

PUBLISHED BY:

HOT OFF THE PRESS INC

For a color catalog of nearly 800 products, send $2.00 to:

HOT OFF THE PRESS INC
1250 N.W. Third, Dept. B
Canby, Oregon 97013
phone (503) 266-9102
fax (503) 266-8749
www.paperpizazz.com

203 PAPER PIECING Patterns

FULL-SIZE PATTERNS READY FOR YOU!

TELEPHONE

London, England

seattle

• Patterns also use eyelets, beads, wire, buttons, etc.

PERFECT FOR:
• scrapbooks
• card making
• bulletin boards

TABLE OF CONTENTS

SUMMER

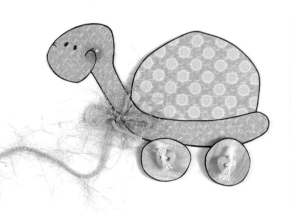

paper piecing is the art of cutting and gluing papers into shapes. It is a great way to add pizazz to your scrapbook pages, cards and other paper crafts. We at Hot Off The Press know how much you love paper piecing and have gathered this collection of 203 patterns for you to enjoy. Simply collect the basic supplies, follow our step-by-step instructions (below) and you'll be ready to make magic. The only difficult step will be deciding which adorable design to make first. We've provided detailed lists of the Paper Pizazz™ patterned papers used in each piece—but, feel free to coordinate designs and colors that compliment your photos and imagination. There are even scrapbook album pages with the finished paper piecing pattern shown to inspire you. Happy paper piecing!

BASIC SUPPLIES

- Paper Pizazz™ patterned, specialty and solid papers (available in books and by the sheet)
- tracing paper
- transfer paper
- pencil
- straight-edged scissors
- paper glue or adhesive
- ruler
- optional supplies: assorted craft punches, foam mounting tape, decorating chalks and applicators, stylus, X-acto® knife and cutting surface

TIPS

- We've provided the Paper Pizazz™ book of papers title in italics for each patterned paper used in every design. When a sheet is available separately, you'll see an asterisk* next to the name of the paper.

- You can enlarge or reduce a pattern simply by using the sizing feature on many photocopiers.

- To get the most out of patterned papers which feature a theme place your tracing paper in a section that captures the best of the design. Our designers used the grain in our barnwood paper for a realistic effect on the "Toolbox."

- Add dimension to your patterns with adhesive foam tape or adhesive dots. Place a small piece of foam tape or a dot behind a nose or fingers that are grabbing onto an item.

- Using lumpy, or three-dimensional, objects on scrapbook pages is so popular now, our designers couldn't resist using them for paper piecing.

- When working with vellum, handle it gently to avoid creases which appear as permanent white lines. Most adhesives will show through vellum, so use it sparingly and apply it to areas where it is layered behind other paper pieces. A glue stick works the best.

- Don't be shy about customizing a design to fit your needs! Combining "Flip Flops" and "Swim Trunks" will frame an album page nicely. Use our specialized Christmas papers with the angel series for holiday theme pages. Also, look for patterns that match your baby's room when creating the baby series of paper piecing patterns. Let your imagine go—we have the papers to match!

HOW TO USE PAPER PIECING PATTERNS

1 Choose your pattern: There are 203 patterns featured in this book for almost any occasion.

2 Choose your papers: We've provided a list of Paper Pizazz™ papers specifically chosen by our designers for each piece. If the colors or patterns won't blend with the colors in your photograph, choose other papers from our extensive selection. The colors should compliment those in your photo, along with the papers used in your scrapbook page.

3 Trace the pattern: Lay a piece of tracing paper over the pattern in this book and use a pencil to go over all the outlines and dotted cutting lines (*there's more about cutting lines in step 7*). You may also want to trace the interior detail lines from the pattern or draw them freehand after the matting process.

4 Transfer the pattern: There are two ways:
• Place the tracing paper on top of your patterned paper. Slip transfer paper underneath the tracing paper and go over the traced lines with a pencil or stylus.
• If you're unsure of transferring the pattern directly onto the patterned paper, flip the tracing paper over and place it on the backside of the patterned paper. Slip transfer paper underneath the tracing paper and go over the lines with a pencil or stylus.

5 Cut out the pattern pieces: A sharp pair of straight-edged scissors are a must, though there are certain designs where decorative-edged scissors or an X-acto® knife can be used. For those small diameter circles and hearts, a paper punch is helpful. We've provided patterns for even the tiniest circles so you don't have to purchase a punch.

6 Mat the pieces: Most of the pattern pieces in this book are matted onto black paper, with a very narrow $\frac{1}{16}$"-$\frac{1}{8}$" wide border (you'll see a red star ★ followed by matting instructions for each project). There are exceptions, though, especially when using vellum or handling very small pieces. Vellum should never be matted to retain its translucent quality. The secret to making it look matted is using a black pen to outline its shape (you'll see a green star ★ followed by penwork instructions for each project). You can use the same pen trick for very small pieces or leave them unmatted.

7 Assemble the pieces: Refer to the color image to arrange the pieces as shown. Some of the pieces will be placed on top of others, so be sure they're placed correctly before gluing them together. A few patterns require inserting part of one piece behind another as shown in the color image.

8 Glue the pieces: Once you're pleased with the design, glue the pieces together. You may want to glue the pattern directly onto your scrapbook page or glue the pieces on a separate piece of paper and trim around the finished profile.

9 Add penwork: Now, you can add detail to your design, such as coloring in the eyes, adding a white highlight to a nose, or drawing in crease marks in a robe. If you're unsure of directly applying pen to your pattern, make light markings with a pencil first. Outlining individual pieces with a pen also adds depth to your pattern.

10 Chalking: One way to add depth and highlight to your pattern is to use decorating chalks. Using them brings out those rosy cheeks on the face of the "Baby on the Moon", depth to the fog around the "Golden Gate Bridge" and highlights to "Snow Lady #1". We've listed the chalk colors with the paper supplies when used by our designers in a pattern piece. Blend it in with a cotton swab or sponge eye shadow applicator.

AIRPLANE

- patterned Paper Pizazz™: red sponged (*Mixing Bright Papers*)
- solid Paper Pizazz™: yellow (*Solid Muted Colors*), black (*Solid Jewel Tones*)
- pewter embossing metal: Art Emboss™
- black brads: HyGlo/American Pin
- black pen: Sakura of America

★ Mat each piece on black as shown

pattern by Annie Lang
pieced by Shauna Berlund-Immel
page by LeNae Gerig

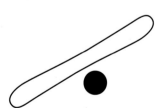

- patterned Paper Pizazz™: blue stars (*Jacie's Watercolor Naturals*), red/blue stripe, red brushed (*Mixing Masculine Papers*)
- specialty Paper Pizazz™: pastel blue vellum (*Vellum Papers,* also by the sheet)
- solid Paper Pizazz™: blue, whie (*12"x12" Solid Pastel Papers*)
- ⅛" silver brads, ½" silver star brads: Magic Scraps™

THE ALAMO

- patterned Paper Pizazz™: southwest brown & turquoise (*Vacation Collage*)
- solid Paper Pizazz™: black (*Solid Jewel Tones*)
- silver beads: Blue Moon Beads/Elizabeth Ward & Co., Inc.
- black wire: Artistic Wire Ltd.
- black pen: Zig® Writer
- adhesive foam tape: Therm O Web

★ Mat each piece on black as shown

pattern by Joy Schaber
pieced by Paris Dukes

ALIEN

- patterned Paper Pizazz™: green paint swirl, blue paint swirl, blue brush stroke, green brush stroke (*Great Jewel Backgrounds*)
- solid Paper Pizazz™: black (*Solid Jewel Tones*), white (*Plain Pastels*)
- green glitter, green shaved ice: Magic Scraps™
- green wire: Artistic Wire Ltd.
- pink, black pens: Sakura of America

★ Mat each piece on black as shown

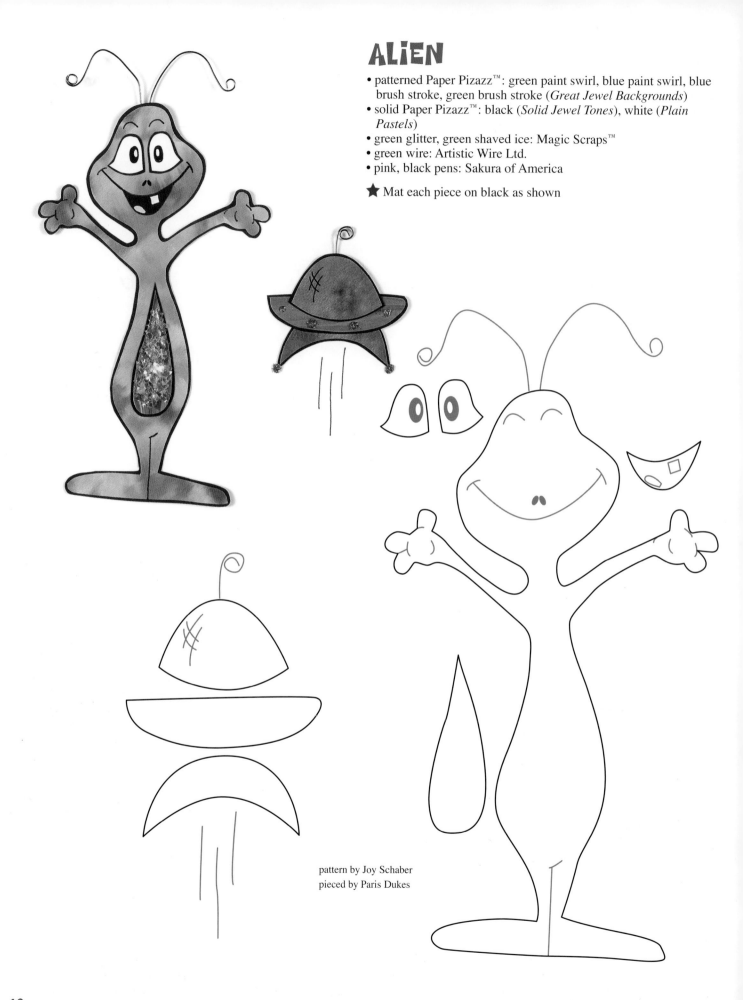

pattern by Joy Schaber
pieced by Paris Dukes

ANCHOR

- specialty Paper Pizazz™: metallic silver* (*Metallic Silver*)
- solid Paper Pizazz™: black (*Solid Jewel Tones*)
- white twisted cording

★ Mat on black as shown

✳ This paper is available by the sheet

pattern by Annie Lang

pieced by Shauna Berlund-Immel

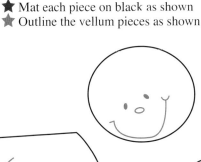

ANGEL DANCING #1

- patterned Paper Pizazz™: pale purple/green gingham, pale purple flowers on green texture, pale purple floral vellum (*Joy's Soft Collection of Papers*)
- solid Paper Pizazz™: black (*Solid Jewel Tones*), ivory, yellow (*Plain Pastels*)
- red, black decorating chalks: Craf-T Products
- red, black, white pens: Sakura Gelly Roll

★ Mat each piece on black as shown

★ Outline the vellum pieces as shown

pattern by Annie Lang

pieced by Shauna Berglund-Immel

11

ANGEL DANCING #2

- patterned Paper Pizazz™: green X's, red X's, green/red plaid (*Mixing Christmas Papers*)
- vellum Paper Pizazz™: pastel green* (*Pastel Vellum Papers*)
- solid Paper Pizazz™: black (*Solid Jewel Tones*), ivory, yellow (*Plain Pastels*)
- gold jingle bells: Westrim® Crafts
- red decorating chalk: Craf-T Products
- black, white pens: Sakura Gelly Roll
- red pen: Zig® Writer
- yellow glitter: Magic Scraps™

★ Mat each piece on black as shown
★ Outline the vellum pieces as shown
✳ This paper is available by the sheet

pattern by Annie Lang
pieced by Shauna Berglund-Immel

ANGEL DANCING #3

- patterned Paper Pizazz™: red criss-cross, blue with red stars, red/white stripes (*Mixing Masculine Papers*)
- solid Paper Pizazz™: black (*Solid Jewel Tones*), ivory, yellow (*Plain Pastels*)
- star button: Dress It Up
- red decorating chalk: Craf-T Products
- black, white pens: Sakura Gelly Roll
- red pen: Zig® Writer
- embossing scroll & brush: Zig®
- gold embossing powder

★ Mat each piece on black as shown

pattern by Annie Lang
pieced by Shauna Berglund-Immel

13

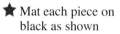

ASIAN CHARACTERS

- patterned Paper Pizazz™: blue with leaves & white floral (*Collage Papers*)
- vellum Paper Pizazz™: pastel blue* (*Pastel Vellum Papers*)
- solid Paper Pizazz™: black (*Solid Jewel Tones*)
- green iridescent beads: Blue Moon Beads/Elizabeth Ward & Co., Inc.
- silver wire: Artistic Wire Ltd.

★ Mat each piece on black as shown
* This paper is available by the sheet

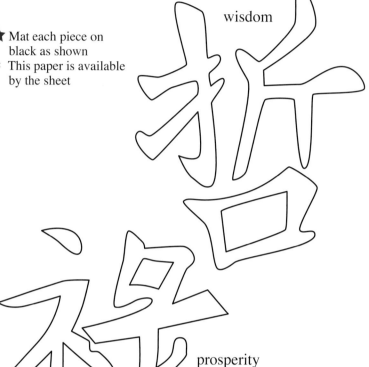

wisdom

prosperity

pieced by Paris Dukes

joy

cut 2 blocks, one for joy, one for wisdom

luck

cut 2 squares, one for luck, one for prosperity

ASIAN SYMBOL #1

- patterned Paper Pizazz™: barnwood*
- specialty Paper Pizazz™: fuchsia/gold floral, metallic gold* (*Metallic Gold*)
- solid Paper Pizazz™: black (*Solid Jewel Tones*)
- metallic gold pen: Pentel Hybrid Gel Rollery

⭐ Mat each piece on black as shown
✳ This paper is available by the sheet

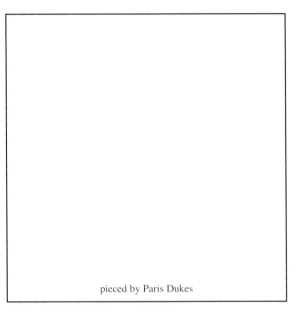

pieced by Paris Dukes

cut 4

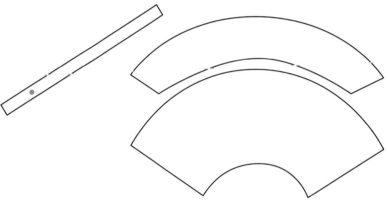

ASIAN SYMBOL #2

- specialty Paper Pizazz™: purple/gold floral, metallic gold* (*Metallic Gold*)
- solid Paper Pizazz™: black (*Solid Jewel Tones*)
- black pen: Zebra Jimnie Gel Rollerball

⭐ Mat each piece on black as shown
✳ This paper is available by the sheet

cut 5

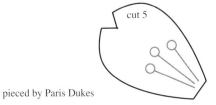

pieced by Paris Dukes

ASIAN SYMBOL #3

- specialty Paper Pizazz™: black/meallic gold floral, metallic gold* (*Metallic Gold*)
- solid Paper Pizazz™: black (*Solid Jewel Tones*)

pieced by Paris Dukes

★ Mat each piece on black as shown
✳ This paper is available by the sheet

cut 3

BABY

- patterned Paper Pizazz™:
  yellow gingham*, pink posies*,
  blue posies*, yellow stripes*
  (*Soft Tints*)
- solid Paper Pizazz™: ivory,
  pink (*Plain Pastels*), black
  (*Solid Jewel Tones*)
- pink, peach decorating chalks: Craf-T
  Products
- black pen: Sakura of America

★ Mat each piece on black as shown
✳ This paper is available by the sheet

pattern by Annie Lang
pieced by Shauna Berglund-Immel

BABY BUGGY

- patterned Paper Pizazz™: lavender texture, pink/blue posies on purple gingham, pink gingham (*Mixing Baby Papers*)
- solid Paper Pizazz™: black (*Solid Jewel Tones*)
- pink, purple decorating chalks: Craf-T Products
- silver heart snaps: Making Memories™
- 20-gauge gunmetal wire: Artistic Wire, Ltd.
- black, white pens: Sakura of America

★ Mat each piece on black as shown

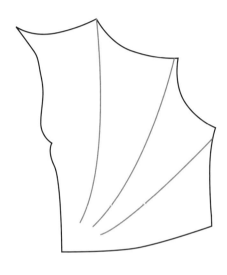

pattern by Annie Lang
pieced by Shauna Berglund-Immel

BABY IN HIGHCHAIR

- patterned Paper Pizazz™: yellow plaid, blue plaid, blue with stars & moons, yellow/blue star stripes (*Mixing Baby Papers*)
- solid Paper Pizazz™: light salmon, light pink (*Plain Pastel Papers*), black (*Solid Jewel Tones*)
- adhesive foam tape: Therm O Web
- white milky gel roller pen: Pentel of America Ltd.
- black pen: Zebra Jimnie

★ Mat each piece on black as shown

BABY

pattern by Joy Schaber
pieced by Paris Dukes

BABY

BABY ON THE MOON

- patterned Paper Pizazz™: yellow plaid, green with pink buttons (*Mixing Baby Papers*)
- solid Paper Pizazz™: yellow, brown (*Solid Muted Colors*), black (*Solid Jewel Tones*), ivory (*Plain Pastels*)
- antique gold thread: DMC
- ⅛" wide pink satin ribbon: C.M. Offray & Son, Inc.
- pink, white, gold, yellow, green decorating chalks: Craf-T Products
- black, white pens: Sakura of America
- salmon pen: Zig® Writer

★ Mat each piece on black as shown

pattern by Annie Lang
pieced by Shauna Berglund-Immel

BALLOON FAMILY

- patterned Paper Pizazz™: pink swirl*, pink diamond*, blue swirl*, blue diamond, yellow swirl*, yellow diamond, green circles (*Bright Tints*)
- solid Paper Pizazz™: black (*Solid Jewel Tones*)
- craft tinsel, glitter: Magic Scraps™
- ⅛" wide satin ribbon: C.M. Offray & Son, Inc.
- pink milky gel roller pen: Pentel of America Ltd.
- black pen: Zebra Jimnie Gel Rollerball

pattern by Annie Lang
pieced by Paris Dukes

★ Mat each piece on black as shown
✻ This paper is available by the sheet

BALLOON WITH CAKE

- patterned Paper Pizazz™: purple swirl, purple stripe, green diamond, green gingham* (*Bright Tints*)
- solid Paper Pizazz™: black (*Solid Jewel Tones*)
- craft tinsel, glitter: Magic Scraps™
- ⅛" wide satin ribbon: C.M. Offray & Son, Inc.
- pink milky gel roller pen: Pentel of America Ltd.
- black pen: Zebra Jimnie Gel Rollerball

★ Mat each piece on black as shown
✻ This paper is available by the sheet

pattern by Annie Lang
pieced by Paris Dukes

BALLOON WITH HORN

- patterned Paper Pizazz™: blue swirl*, blue circles, yellow diamond (*Bright Tints*)
- solid Paper Pizazz™: black (*Solid Jewel Tones*)
- craft tinsel, glitter: Magic Scraps™
- ⅛" wide satin ribbon: C.M. Offray & Son, Inc.
- pink milky gel roller pen: Pentel of America Ltd.
- black pen: Zebra Jimnie Gel Rollerball

★ Mat each piece on black as shown
✳ This paper is available by the sheet

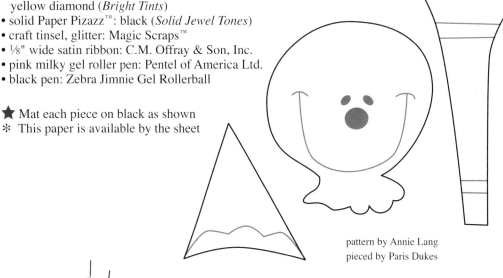

pattern by Annie Lang
pieced by Paris Dukes

BALLOON WITH PRESENT

- patterned Paper Pizazz™: pink swirl*, pink diamond, green diamond (*Bright Tints*)
- solid Paper Pizazz™: black (*Solid Jewel Tones*)
- craft tinsel, glitter: Magic Scraps™
- ⅛" wide satin ribbon: C.M. Offray & Son, Inc.
- pink milky gel roller pen: Pentel of America Ltd.
- black pen: Zebra Jimnie Gel Rollerball

★ Mat each piece on black as shown
✳ This paper is available by the sheet

pattern by Annie Lang
pieced by Paris Dukes

BASEBALL & BAT

- patterned Paper Pizazz™: barnwood*
- solid Paper Pizazz™: black (*Solid Jewel Tones*), ivory (*Plain Pastels*)
- black pen: Zebra Jimnie Gel Rollerball

★ Mat each piece on black as shown
✳ This paper is available by the sheet

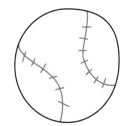

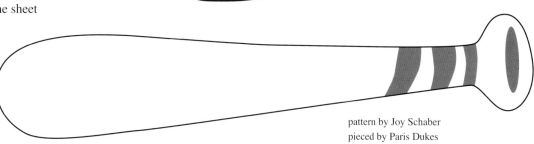

pattern by Joy Schaber
pieced by Paris Dukes

BEAR

- patterned Paper Pizazz™: tan speckled (*Soft & Subtle Textures*), crushed suede* (*For Black & White Photos*)
- solid Paper Pizazz™: black (*Solid Jewel Tones*)
- button, ⅝" wide sheer green gingham ribbon: Magic Scraps™
- black pen: Zebra Jimnie Gel Rollerball
- adhesive foam tape: Therm O Web

pattern by Joy Schaber
pieced by Paris Dukes

★ Mat each piece on black as shown
✱ This paper is available by the sheet

cut 2

BEE

- patterned Paper Pizazz™: yellow dots* (*Soft Tints*)
- solid Paper Pizazz™: black (*Solid Jewel Tones*), pink (*Plain Pastels*)
- vellum Paper Pizazz™: white* (*Vellum Papers*)
- pink, blue decorating chalks: Craf-T Products
- 24-gauge black wire: ColourCraft™
- black pen: Sakura Gelly Roll

★ Outline the vellum pieces as shown
✱ This paper is available by the sheet

pattern by Annie Lang
pieced by Shauna Berglund-Immel

BEER STEIN

- patterned Paper Pizazz™: yellow dots*, yellow wavy line (*Soft Tints*)
- vellum Paper Pizazz™: white* (*Vellum Papers*)
- tiny glass beads: Magic Scraps™
- black pen: Zebra Jimnie Gel Rollerball

pattern by Jacie Pete
pieced by Paris Dukes

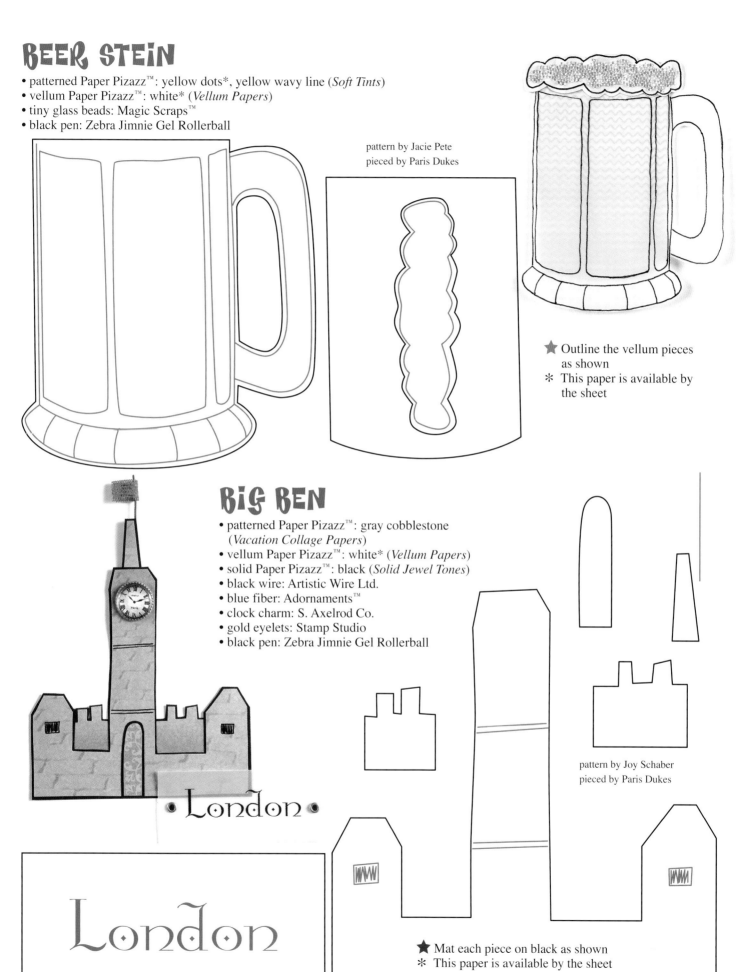

⭐ Outline the vellum pieces as shown

✳ This paper is available by the sheet

BIG BEN

- patterned Paper Pizazz™: gray cobblestone (*Vacation Collage Papers*)
- vellum Paper Pizazz™: white* (*Vellum Papers*)
- solid Paper Pizazz™: black (*Solid Jewel Tones*)
- black wire: Artistic Wire Ltd.
- blue fiber: Adornaments™
- clock charm: S. Axelrod Co.
- gold eyelets: Stamp Studio
- black pen: Zebra Jimnie Gel Rollerball

pattern by Joy Schaber
pieced by Paris Dukes

⭐ Mat each piece on black as shown

✳ This paper is available by the sheet

London

London

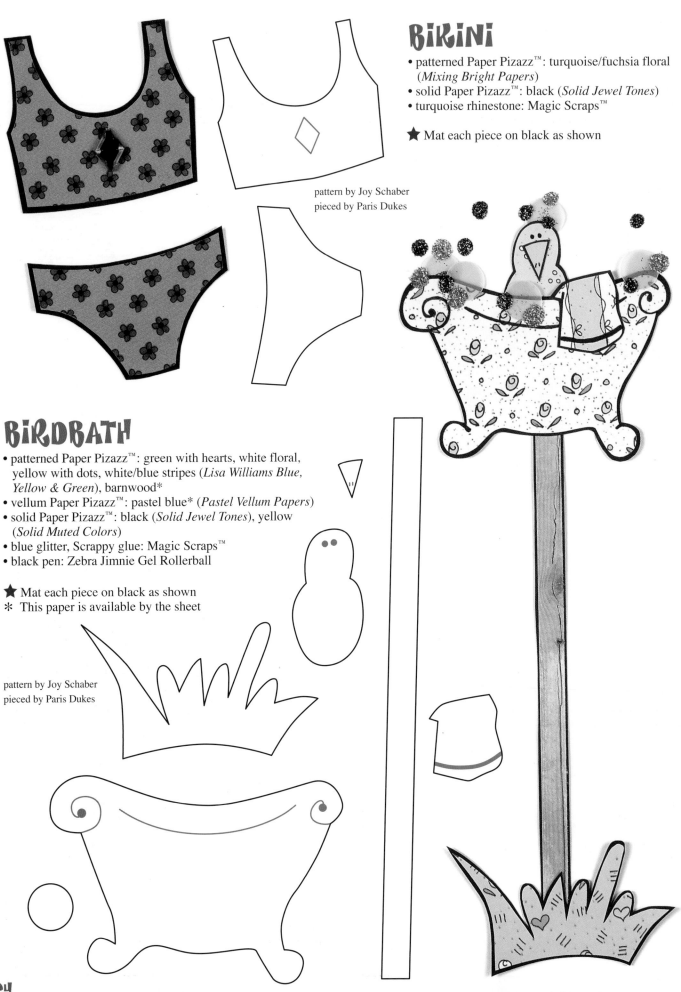

BIKINI

- patterned Paper Pizazz™: turquoise/fuchsia floral (*Mixing Bright Papers*)
- solid Paper Pizazz™: black (*Solid Jewel Tones*)
- turquoise rhinestone: Magic Scraps™

★ Mat each piece on black as shown

pattern by Joy Schaber
pieced by Paris Dukes

BIRDBATH

- patterned Paper Pizazz™: green with hearts, white floral, yellow with dots, white/blue stripes (*Lisa Williams Blue, Yellow & Green*), barnwood*
- vellum Paper Pizazz™: pastel blue* (*Pastel Vellum Papers*)
- solid Paper Pizazz™: black (*Solid Jewel Tones*), yellow (*Solid Muted Colors*)
- blue glitter, Scrappy glue: Magic Scraps™
- black pen: Zebra Jimnie Gel Rollerball

★ Mat each piece on black as shown
✳ This paper is available by the sheet

pattern by Joy Schaber
pieced by Paris Dukes

BIRDHOUSES

- patterned Paper Pizazz™: yellow swirl* (*Bright Tints*), Best Buds*, Girl Power* (*A Girl's Scrapbook*), barnwood*, blue swirls*, grass*
- solid Paper Pizazz™: black (*Solid Jewel Tones*), yellow (*Solid Muted Colors*), green (*Plain Brights*)
- black pen: Zebra Jimnie Gel Rollerball

★ Mat each piece on black as shown
✳ This paper is available by the sheet

cut 4

pattern by Joy Schaber
pieced by Paris Dukes

BIRTHDAY CAKE

- patterned Paper Pizazz™: pink floral, green/pink plaid, green dot (*Mixing Soft Patterned Papers*)
- vellum Paper Pizazz™: pastel pink* (*Pastel Vellum Papers*)
- solid Paper Pizazz™: pink (*Plain Pastels*)
- glitter: Magic Scraps™
- black pen: Zebra Jimnie Gel Rollerball

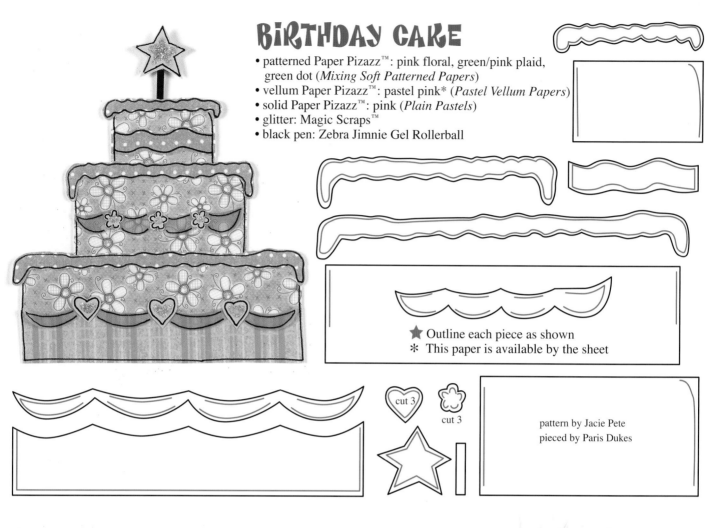

★ Outline each piece as shown
✱ This paper is available by the sheet

cut 3
cut 3

pattern by Jacie Pete
pieced by Paris Dukes

BLUEBIRD

- patterned Paper Pizazz™: green swirl, blue floral (*Muted Tints*) blue speckle (*Lisa Williams Blue, Yellow & Green*), beige speckle (*Lisa Williams Pink, Lavender & Beige*)
- solid Paper Pizazz™: black (*Solid Jewel Tones*)
- blue feather: Zucker Feather Products
- black pen: Zebra Jimnie Gel Rollerball

★ Mat each piece on black as shown

pattern by Annie Lang
pieced by Paris Dukes

BOOTS

- patterned Paper Pizazz™: brown leather, green/brown flannel, green/brown leather (*Mixing Masculine Papers*)
- solid Paper Pizazz™: black (*Solid Jewel Tones*)
- ⅛" gold brads: Magic Scraps™
- black embroidery floss: DMC
- hemp twine: Darice
- black pen: Sakura Gelly Roll

⭐ Mat each piece on black as shown

pattern by Joy Schaber
pieced by Shauna Berglund-Immel

BORDER, BALLOONS

- vellum Paper Pizazz™: pastel green*, pastel yellow*, pastel pink*, pastel purple*, pastel blue* (*Pastel Vellum Papers*), blue dot, purple hearts, green swirl, mauve floral (*Colored Vellum Papers*)
- pink, lavender, yellow, mint green embroidery floss: DMC
- ⅛" wide pink satin ribon: C.M. Offray & Son, Inc.
- black pen: Zebra Jimnie Gel Rollerball
- white pen: Pentel Milky Lunar Gel Roller
- mounting adhesive: Therm O Web

⭐ Outline each piece with black as shown
✳ This paper is available by the sheet

cut 5

cut 4

pattern by Jacie Pete
pieced by Paris Dukes

BORDER, BOWS

- patterned Paper Pizazz™: purple floral border, purple floral vellum (*Mixing Papers & Vellums*)
- black pen: Zebra Jimnie Gel Rollerball
- adhesive foam tape: Therm O Web

⭐ Outline the bows as shown

pattern by Jacie Pete
pieced by Paris Dukes

cut 3

cut 2

cut 3

cut 3

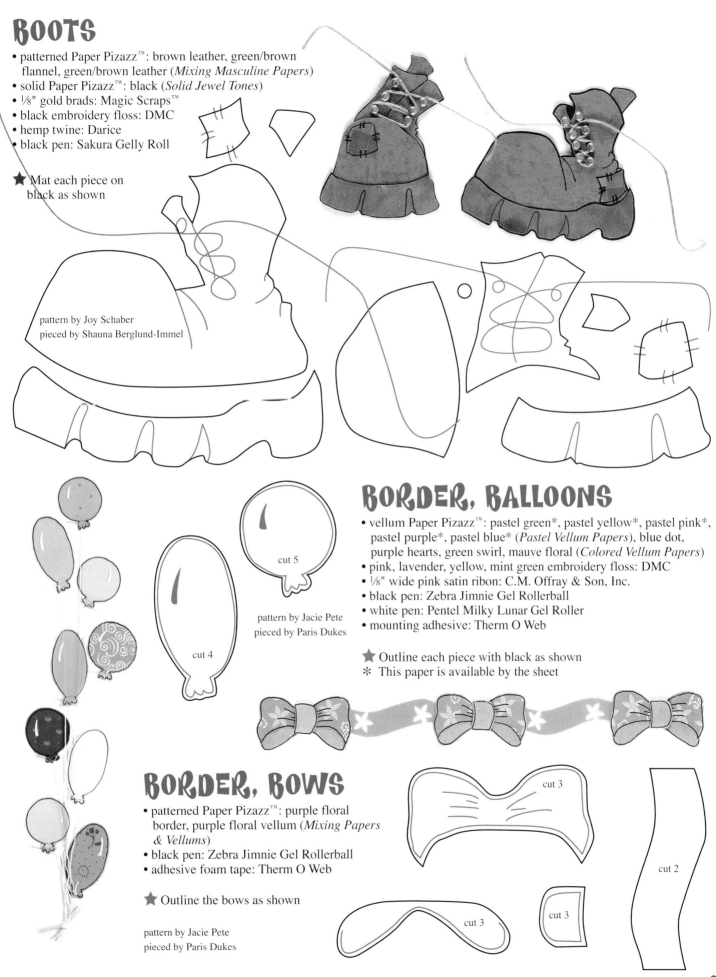

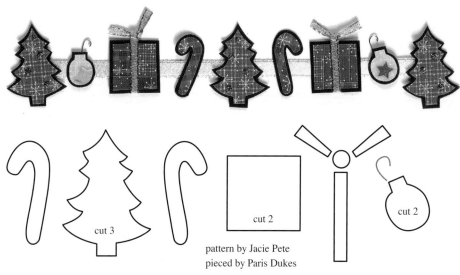

BORDER, CHRISTMAS

- patterned Paper Pizazz™: patchwork with Santa border, red snowflake plaid, green snowflake plaid, gold plaid with stars (*Mixing Christmas Papers*)
- solid Paper Pizazz™: black (*Solid Jewel Tones*)
- gold wire: ColourCraft™
- gold glitter: Magic Scraps™
- ⅛" wide gold ribbon: C.M. Offray & Son, Inc.
- ¼" wide gold ribbon: Ribbon Bowtique

⭐ Mat each piece on black as shown

cut 3

cut 2

cut 2

pattern by Jacie Pete
pieced by Paris Dukes

BORDER, CHRISTMAS LIGHTS

- specialty Paper Pizazz™: pastel pink vellum*, pastel green vellum*, pastel yellow vellum*, pastel purple vellum*, pastel blue vellum*, (*Pastel Vellum Papers*), metallic gold*, (*Metallic Gold*)
- solid Paper Pizazz™: black (*Solid Jewel Tones*)
- gold wire: ColourCraft™
- red, green, yellow, purple, blue decorating chalks: Craf-T Products
- black pen: Zebra Jimnie Gel Rollerball
- white pen: Pentel Milky Lunar Gel Roller

⭐ Mat each gold piece on black as shown
⭐ Outline the vellum pieces as shown
✳ This paper is available by the sheet

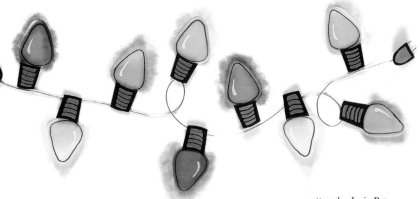

pattern by Jacie Pete
pieced by Paris Dukes

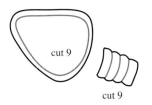
cut 9

cut 9

cut 2

BORDER, FLOWERS

- patterned Paper Pizazz™: black with daisies, fuchsia/teal plaid, teal leaves (*Mixing Jewel Patterned Papers*)
- solid Paper Pizazz™: black (*Solid Jewel Tones*)
- silver flower snaps: Making Memories™ Details™
- silver eyelets: Stamp Studio
- black wire: Artistic Wire Ltd.

⭐ Mat each piece on black as shown

pattern by Jacie Pete
pieced by Paris Dukes

cut 5

cut 10

cut 4

BORDER, HEARTS

- patterned Paper Pizazz™: pink plaid, pink with hearts and "Love, Laughter & Happiness" (*Mixing Light Papers*)
- solid Paper Pizazz™: black (*Solid Jewel Tones*)
- ⅝" wide sheer black ribbon, ⅞" wide sheer pink ribbon: Sheer Creations

pattern by Jacie Pete
pieced by Paris Dukes

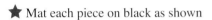

★ Mat each piece on black as shown

BOWS

- patterned Paper Pizazz™: sunflowers, green/gold plaid (*Coordinating Florals & Patterns*)
- solid Paper Pizazz™: black (*Solid Jewel Tones*)
- raffia: Darice
- black pen: Zebra Jimnie Gel Rollerball
- adhesive foam tape: Therm O Web

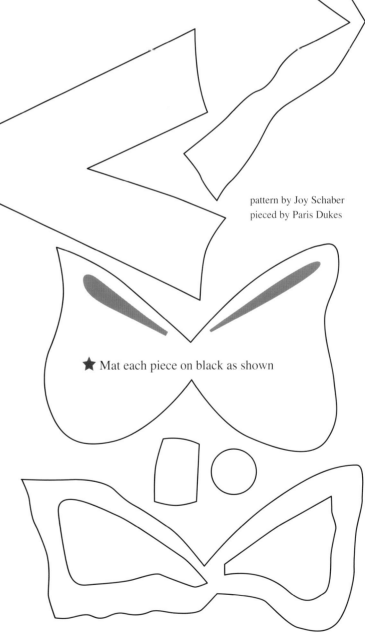

pattern by Joy Schaber
pieced by Paris Dukes

★ Mat each piece on black as shown

BOY & DOG FISHING

- patterned Paper Pizazz™: green cabin, blue fishing (*Masculine Collage*), peach/tan sponged (*Mixing Light Papers*), tan speckled (*Soft & Subtle Textures*), crushed suede* (*For Black & White Photos*), pink swirl (*Great Jewel Backgrounds*), barnwood*
- solid Paper Pizazz™: light salmon (*Plain Pastel Papers*), black (*Solid Jewel Tones*)
- hemp twine: Darice
- pink decorating chalk: Craf-T Products
- red bead: Magic Scraps™
- black pen: Zebra Jimmie Gel Rollerball

★ Mat each piece on black as shown
✳ This paper is available by the sheet

pattern by Annie Lang
pieced by Paris Dukes

BOY FISHING #1

- patterned Paper Pizazz™: green cabin, blue fishing (*Masculine Collage*), purple swirl (*Great Jewel Backgrounds*), brown tropical (*Vacation Collage*), barnwood*, crushed suede* (*For Black & White Photos*), denim*
- specialty Paper Pizazz™: metallic silver* (*Metallic Silver*)
- solid Paper Pizazz™: light salmon (*Plain Pastel Papers*), black (*Solid Jewel Tones*)
- 20-gauge black, silver wire: Artistic Wire Ltd.
- pink decorating chalk: Craf-T Products
- silver snap: Making Memories™
- black pen: Zebra Jimnie Gel Rollerball

★ Mat each piece on black as shown
✳ This paper is available by the sheet

pattern by Annie Lang
pieced by Paris Dukes

BOY FISHING #2

- patterned Paper Pizazz™: brown tropical (*Masculine Collage*), purple swirl (*Great Jewel Backgrounds*), red/black plaid*, denim*, barnwood*, crushed suede* (*For Black & White Photos*)
- solid Paper Pizazz™: light salmon (*Plain Pastel Papers*), black (*Solid Jewel Tones*)
- 20-gauge black wire: Artistic Wire Ltd.
- pink pen: Pentel Milky Gel Roller
- black pen: Zebra Jimnie Gel Rollerball

★ Mat each piece on black as shown
✷ This paper is available by the sheet

cut 3

rear foot

pattern by Annie Lang
pieced by Paris Dukes

BOY FISHING #3

- patterned Paper Pizazz™: purple mosaic (*Soft & Subtle Textures*), red/black plaid,* denim,* barnwood*, crushed suede* (*For Black & White Photos*), grass,* pool water*
- solid Paper Pizazz™: light salmon, white (*Plain Pastel Papers*)
- gold button: Magic Scraps™
- pink decorating chalk: Craf-T Products
- hemp twine: Darice
- black pen: Zebra Jimnie Gel Rollerball

★ Outline each piece with black as shown
✳ This paper is available by the sheet

pattern by Annie Lang
pieced by Paris Dukes

BOY READING

- patterned Paper Pizazz™: blue texture, blue with green dots, blue/yellow checks (*Mixing Baby Papers*), tan speckle (*Soft & Subtle Textures*), denim*
- solid Paper Pizazz™: light salmon (*Plain Pastel Papers*), white (*Plain Pastels*)
- gold button: Magic Scraps™
- pink decorating chalk: Craf-T Products
- black pen: Zebra Jimnie Gel Rollerball

★ Outline each piece with black as shown
✳ This paper is available by the sheet

pattern by Annie Lang
pieced by Paris Dukes

BRITISH TELEPHONE BOOTH

- patterned Paper Pizazz™: red with hollow dots*, red/black checks*
- vellum Paper Pizazz™: white* (*Vellum Papers*)
- solid Paper Pizazz™: red, black (*Solid Jewel Tones*)
- black pen: Zebra Jimnie Gel Rollerball

★ Mat each piece on black as shown
✴ This paper is available by the sheet

TELEPHONE

London, England

pattern by Joy Schaber
pieced by Paris Dukes

BUCKET LOADER

- patterned Paper Pizazz™: yellow circles, yellow checks (*Bright Tints*)
- specialty Paper Pizazz™: white vellum* (*Vellum Papers*), metallic silver* (*Metallic Silver*)
- solid Paper Pizazz™: black (*Solid Jewel Tones*)
- black pen: Zebra Jimnie Gel Rollerball

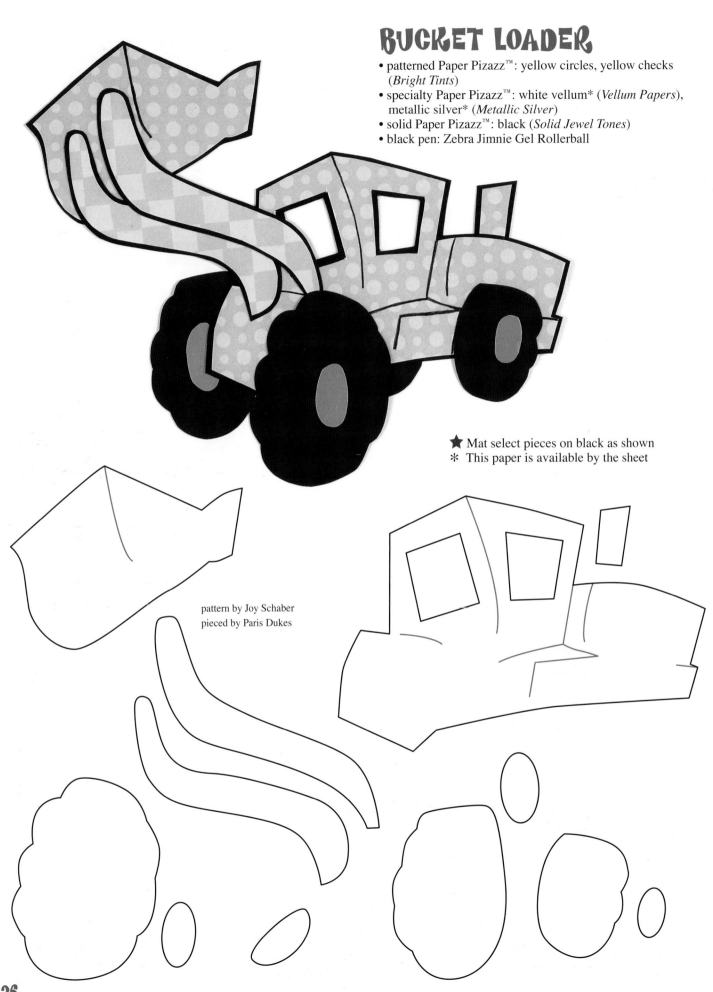

★ Mat select pieces on black as shown
✳ This paper is available by the sheet

pattern by Joy Schaber
pieced by Paris Dukes

BUG JAR

- patterned Paper Pizazz™: green swirls, pink/purple sponged, red sponged (*Great Jewel Backgrounds*), grass*
- vellum Paper Pizazz™: white* (*Vellum Papers*), pastel blue* (*Pastel Vellum Papers*)
- solid Paper Pizazz™: black (*Solid Jewel Tones*), white (*Plain Pastels*), yellow (*Solid Muted Colors*)
- pewter emobssing metal: ArtEmboss™
- black pen: Sakura Gelly Roll

★ Mat select pieces on black as shown
★ Outline the vellum pieces as shown
✳ This paper is available by the sheet

- patterned Paper Pizazz™: blue swirl, green gingham (*Bright Tints*, also by the sheet), blue dot, green dot (*Bright Tints*)
- specialty Paper Pizazz™: white vellum (*Vellum Papers*, also by the sheet), pastel purple vellum (*Pastel Vellum Papers*, also by the sheet)
- solid Paper Pizazz™: pastel purple (*Plain Pastels*)
- Paper Pizazz™ Cut-Outs™: dragonfly, lady bugs (*Vellum Cut-Outs*™)
- Fat Caps alphabet template: Francis Meyers, Inc.
- lavender, green fibers: Adornments™

**Attention Paper Piecers!
The projects in this book
make great art for tags!**

pattern by Annie Lang
pieced by Shauna Berglund-Immel
page by LeNae Gerig

BUNNY IN HALF AN EGG

- patterned Paper Pizazz™: green/blue stripes, green with pink buttons, blue sponged, multi-color floral, pink gingham (*Mixing Baby Papers*)
- solid Paper Pizazz™: black (*Solid Jewel Tones*)
- black pen: Zebra Jimnie Gel Rollerball
- white pen: Sakura Gelly Roll
- adhesive foam tape: Therm O Web

★ Mat each piece on black as shown

pattern by Joy Schaber
pieced by Paris Dukes

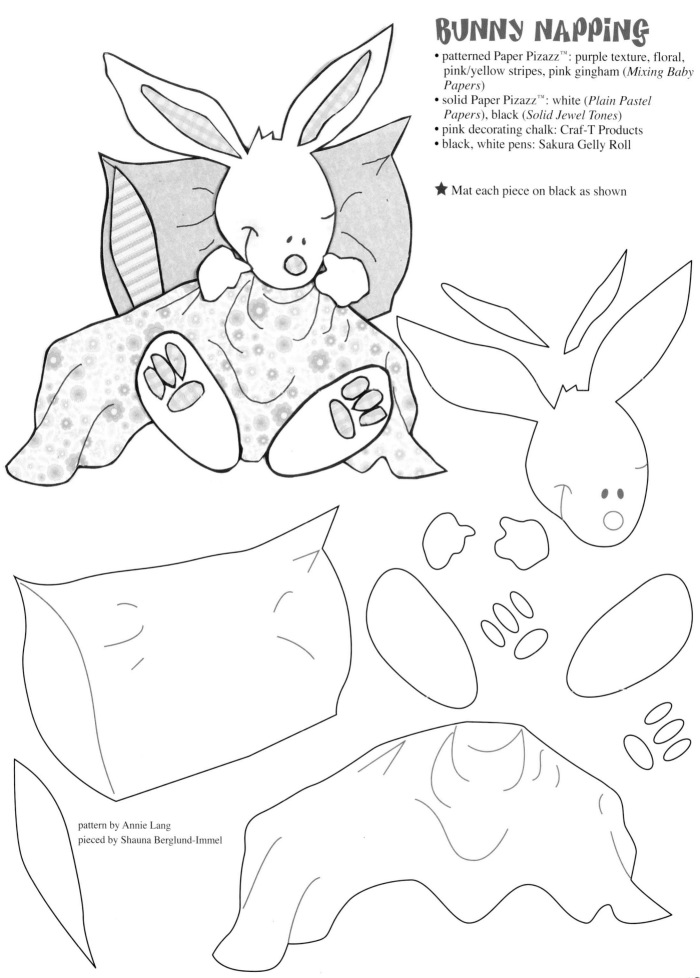

BUNNY NAPPING

- patterned Paper Pizazz™: purple texture, floral, pink/yellow stripes, pink gingham (*Mixing Baby Papers*)
- solid Paper Pizazz™: white (*Plain Pastel Papers*), black (*Solid Jewel Tones*)
- pink decorating chalk: Craf-T Products
- black, white pens: Sakura Gelly Roll

★ Mat each piece on black as shown

pattern by Annie Lang
pieced by Shauna Berglund-Immel

BUNNY SLIPPER

- patterned Paper Pizazz™: blue texture, pink gingham (*Mixing Baby Papers*)
- pink decorating chalk: Craf-T Products
- black pen: Zebra Jimnie Gel Rollerball

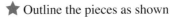

★ Outline the pieces as shown

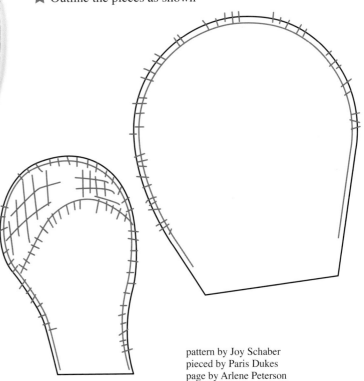

pattern by Joy Schaber
pieced by Paris Dukes
page by Arlene Peterson

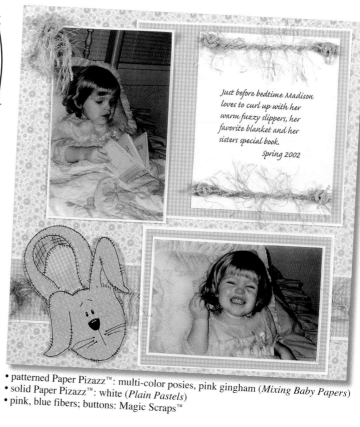

Just before bedtime Madison loves to curl up with her warm fuzzy slippers, her favorite blanket and her sisters special book.

Spring 2002

- patterned Paper Pizazz™: multi-color posies, pink gingham (*Mixing Baby Papers*)
- solid Paper Pizazz™: white (*Plain Pastels*)
- pink, blue fibers; buttons: Magic Scraps™

BUSHEL OF APPLES

- patterned Paper Pizazz™: red crosshatch (*Mixing Masculine Papers*), barnwood*
- solid Paper Pizazz™: black (*Solid Jewel Tones*)
- black wire: Artistic Wire Ltd.
- black pen: Zebra Jimmie Gel Rollerball

★ Mat each piece on black as shown
✳ This paper is available by the sheet

pattern by Joy Schaber
pieced by Paris Dukes

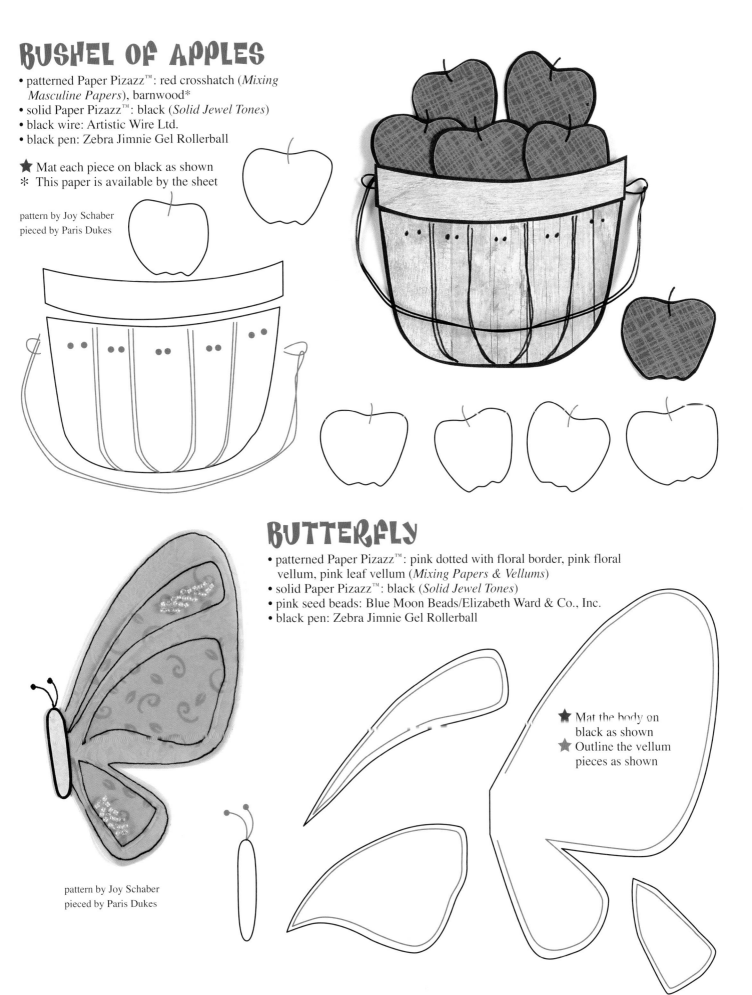

BUTTERFLY

- patterned Paper Pizazz™: pink dotted with floral border, pink floral vellum, pink leaf vellum (*Mixing Papers & Vellums*)
- solid Paper Pizazz™: black (*Solid Jewel Tones*)
- pink seed beads: Blue Moon Beads/Elizabeth Ward & Co., Inc.
- black pen: Zebra Jimmie Gel Rollerball

★ Mat the body on black as shown
★ Outline the vellum pieces as shown

pattern by Joy Schaber
pieced by Paris Dukes

CACTUS

- patterned Paper Pizazz™: green road signs, brown southwest, blue southwest (*Vacation Collage*)
- solid Paper Pizazz™: black (*Solid Jewel Tones*)
- silver, turquoise seed beads: Blue Moon Beads/ Elizabeth Ward & Co., Inc.
- wire: Artistic Wire Ltd.
- black pen: Sakura Gelly Roll

★ Mat each piece on black as shown

pattern by Joy Schaber
pieced by Paris Dukes

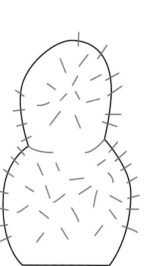

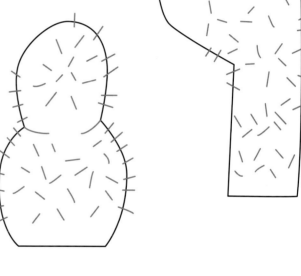

CANADIAN FLAG

- red, cream Twistel™: Making Memories™
- black pen: Sakura Gelly Roll

cut 2

pieced by Shauna Berglund-Immel

O Canada

O Canada

CAR, COMPACT

- patterned Paper Pizazz™: girl power* (*A Girl's Scrapbook*)
- specialty Paper Pizazz™: white vellum* (*Vellum Papers*), metallic silver* (*Metallic Silver*)
- solid Paper Pizazz™: white (*Plain Pastel Papers*), black (*Solid Jewel Tones*)
- rhinestone: Westrim® Crafts
- 20-gauge black wire: Artistic Wire Ltd.
- white flower eyelets: Making Memories™
- blue decorating chalk: Craf-T Products
- black, white pens: Sakura Gelly Roll

cut 2

⭐ Mat select pieces on black as shown
⭐ Outline/Highlight the vellum piece with black and white as shown
✳ This paper is available by the sheet

pattern by Annie Lang
pieced by Shauna Berglund-Immel

CAR, ROADSTER

- patterned Paper Pizazz™: black satin, red with black & white dots with floral border (*Heritage Papers*)
- specialty Paper Pizazz™: white vellum* (*Vellum Papers*), metallic silver* (*Metallic Silver*)
- solid Paper Pizazz™: white (*Plain Pastel Papers*), black (*Solid Jewel Tones*)
- silver snap: Making Memories™
- black pen: Zebra Jimnie Gel Rollerball

★ Mat select pieces on black as shown
★ Outline the vellum with black as shown
✳ This paper is available by the sheet

pattern by Joy Schaber
pieced by Paris Dukes
page by Arlene Peterson

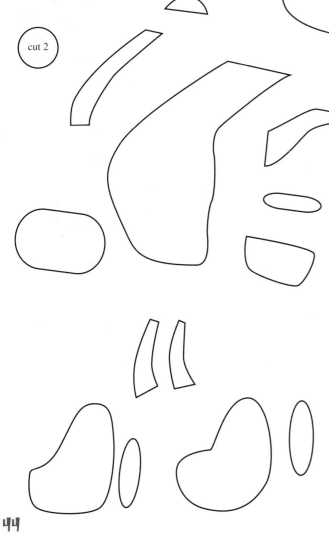

cut 2

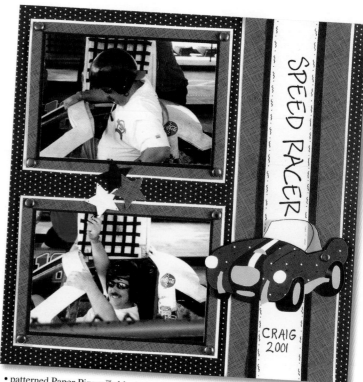

- patterned Paper Pizazz™: black dot (by the sheet), red scratches (*Mixing Masculine Papers*)
- solid Paper Pizazz™: white (*Plain Pastels*), black (*Solid Jewel Tones*)
- ¼" silver brads: Magic Scraps™
- 1⅛" star punch: McGill, Inc.

CAR, SEDAN

- patterned Paper Pizazz™: purple sponged, blue strokes (*Mixing Heritage Papers*)
- specialty Paper Pizazz™: white vellum* (*Vellum Papers*), metallic silver* (*Metallic Silver*)
- solid Paper Pizazz™: white (*Plain Pastel Papers*), black (*Solid Jewel Tones*)
- silver embossing metal: ArtEmboss™
- black pen: Sakura of America

★ Mat select pieces on black as shown
★ Outline the vellum with black as shown
✳ This paper is available by the sheet

pattern by Annie Lang
pieced by Shauna Berglund-Immel
page by LeNae Gerig

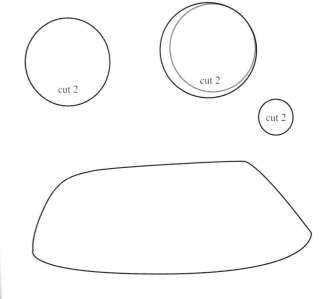

cut 2

cut 2

cut 2

- patterned Paper Pizazz™: lavender swirls (*Soft Tints*, also by the sheet), blue stripes (*Mixing Masculine Papers*)
- vellum Paper Pizazz™: pastel purple, pastel blue (*Pastel Vellum Papers*, also by the sheet)
- solid Paper Pizazz™: white, blue (*Plain Pastels*)
- ⅛" eyelets: Magic Scraps™
- ½", 1½" circle punches: Marvy® Uchida

CHERRIES

- patterned Paper Pizazz™: red swirl, green wavy gingham (*Jewel Tints*)
- solid Paper Pizazz™: black (*Solid Jewel Tones*)

★ Mat each piece on black as shown

pattern by Jacie Pete
pieced by Paris Dukes

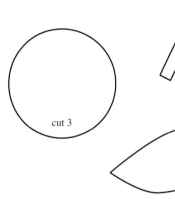

cut 3

CHILD IN SLEEPING BAG

- patterned Paper Pizazz™: red/yellow mesh*, red plaid (*Bright Tints*), barnwood*
- solid Paper Pizazz™: white, light salmon (*Plain Pastel Papers*), black (*Solid Jewel Tones*)
- rose decorating chalk: Craf-T Products
- black, white, red pens: Sakura Gelly Roll

★ Mat each piece on black as shown
✻ This paper is available by the sheet

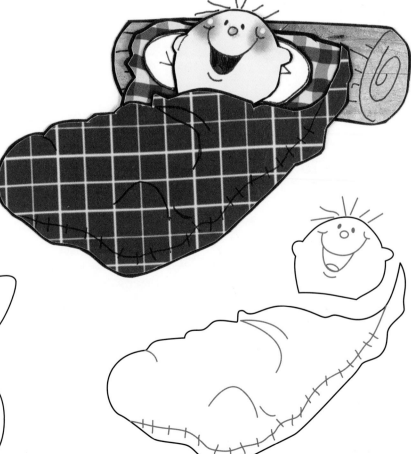

pattern by Annie Lang
pieced by Shauna Berglund-Immel

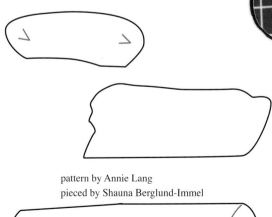

CHILD IN TENT

- patterned Paper Pizazz™: leaf & swirls, burgundy with branches (*Mixing Jewel Patterned Papers*), green log cabin (*Masculine Collage*), tan speckle (*Soft & Subtle Textures*), tan/peach sponged (*Mixing Light Papers*), grass*, denim*
- specialty Paper Pizazz™: white vellum* (*Vellum Papers*), metallic gold* (*Metallic Gold*)
- solid Paper Pizazz™: white, light salmon (*Plain Pastel Papers*)
- fibers: Adornaments™
- gold snaps: Making Memories™
- yellow, pink decorating chalks: Craf-T Products
- light orange pen: Pentel Milky Gel Roller
- black pen: Sakura Gelly Roll

★ Outline each piece with black as shown

✳ This paper is available by the sheet

pattern by Annie Lang
pieced by Paris Dukes

47

CHRISTMAS CANDLES

- patterned Paper Pizazz™: red/green/gold plaid, gold feathers (*Mixing Christmas Papers*)
- specialty Paper Pizazz™: metallic gold* (*Metallic Gold*), ivory vellum*
- solid Paper Pizazz™: black (*Solid Jewel Tones*)
- gold glitter: Magic Scraps™
- black pen: Zebra Jimnie Gel Rollerball

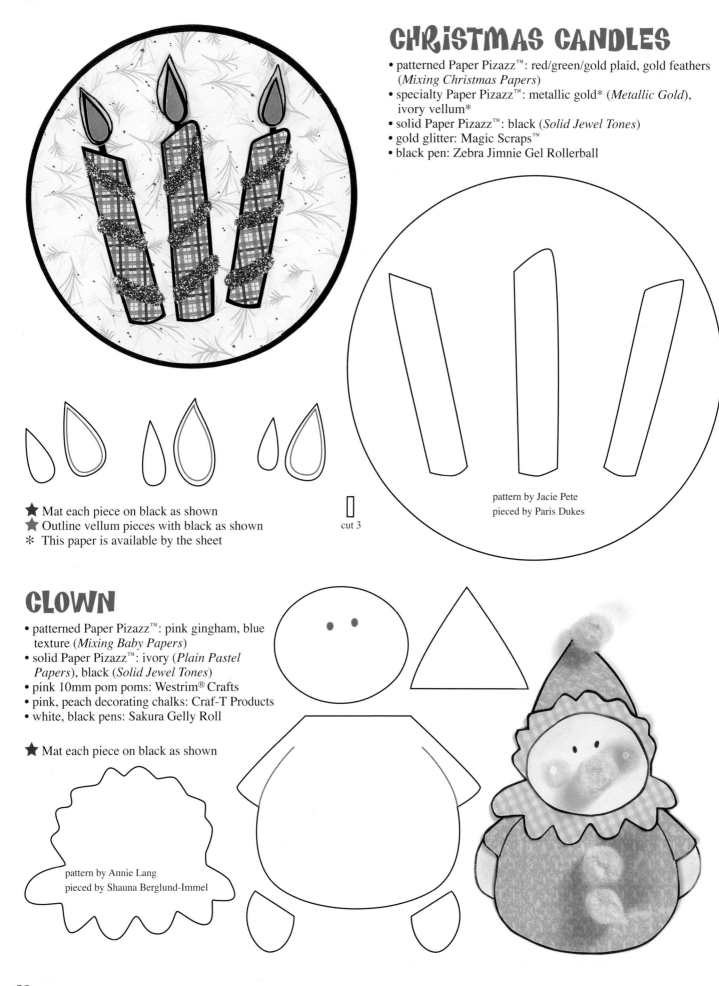

⭐ Mat each piece on black as shown
⭐ Outline vellum pieces with black as shown
✻ This paper is available by the sheet

cut 3

pattern by Jacie Pete
pieced by Paris Dukes

CLOWN

- patterned Paper Pizazz™: pink gingham, blue texture (*Mixing Baby Papers*)
- solid Paper Pizazz™: ivory (*Plain Pastel Papers*), black (*Solid Jewel Tones*)
- pink 10mm pom poms: Westrim® Crafts
- pink, peach decorating chalks: Craf-T Products
- white, black pens: Sakura Gelly Roll

⭐ Mat each piece on black as shown

pattern by Annie Lang
pieced by Shauna Berglund-Immel

CLUBHOUSE

- patterned Paper Pizazz™: red/white stripes with stars (*Mixing Heritage Papers*), gold sponged stars* (*A Woman's Scrapbook*), barnwood*, grass*
- solid Paper Pizazz™: black (*Solid Jewel Tones*)
- 24-gauge black wire: Artistic Wire Ltd.
- peach, red decorating chalks: Craf-T Products
- silver eyelets: HyGlo/American Pin
- salmon pen: Zig® Writer
- white, black pens: Sakura Gelly Roll
- adhesive foam tape: Therm O Web

★ Mat each piece on black as shown
✳ This paper is available by the sheet

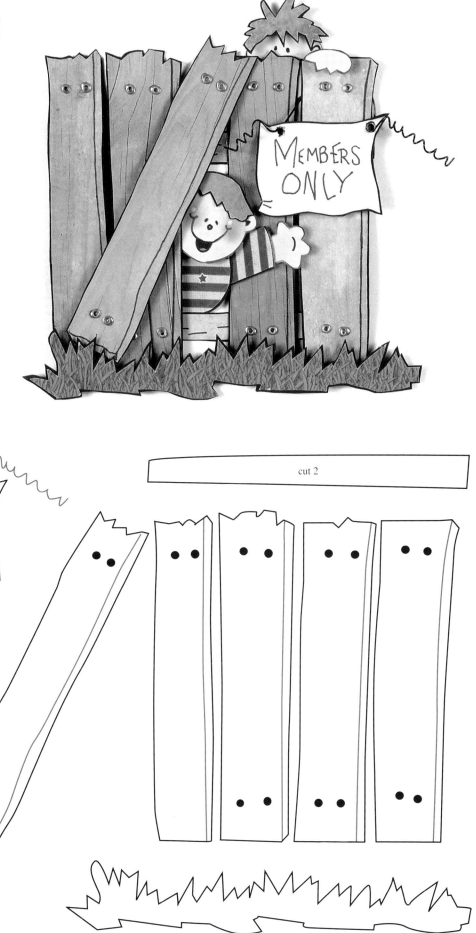

MEMBERS ONLY

cut 2

pattern by Annie Lang
pieced by Shauna Berglund-Immel

CORNUCOPIA

- patterned Paper Pizazz™: brown texture (*Flowered "Handmade Papers"*)
- solid Paper Pizazz™: black, purple, green, brown, orange (*Solid Jewel Tones*), white, ivory (*Plain Pastels*)
- raffia
- orange, yellow decorating calks: Craf-T Products
- black pen: Zebra Jimnie Gel Rollerball
- white pen: Sakura Gelly Roll

★ Mat each piece on black as shown

pattern by Annie Lang
pieced by Paris Dukes

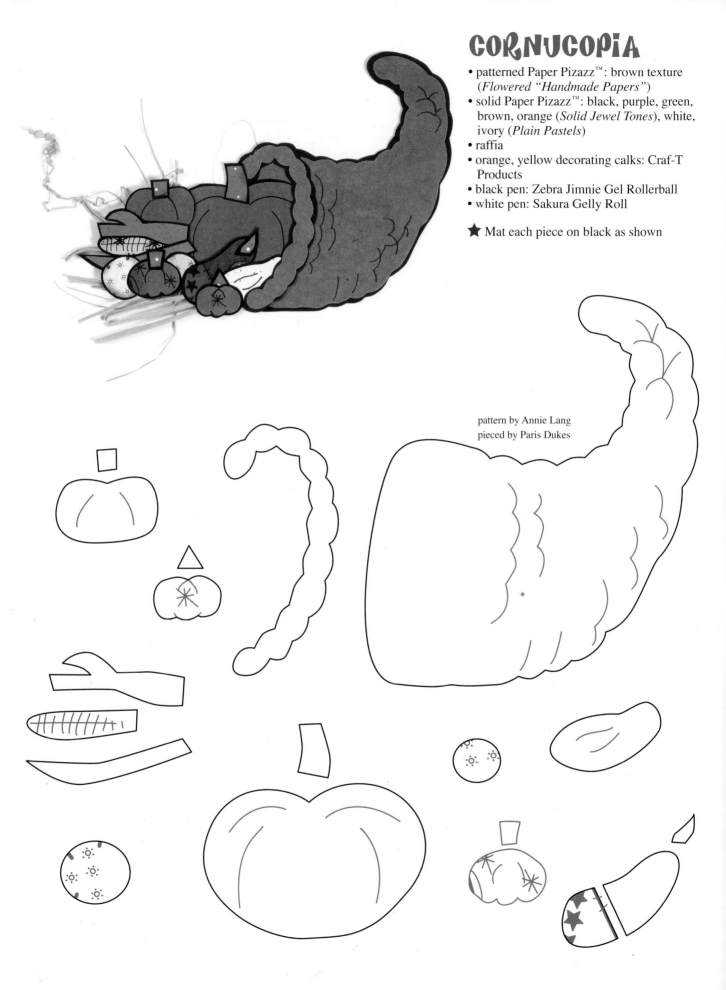

COUPLE DANCING

- patterned Paper Pizazz™: blue with tiny flowers, blue/purple/aqua stripe, purple/blue texture (*Mixing Heritage Papers*), crushed suede* (*For Black & White Photos*)
- solid Paper Pizazz™: ivory (*Plain Pastel Papers*), black (*Solid Jewel Tones*)
- purple fibers: Adornaments™
- pink decorating chalk: Craf-T Products
- black pen: Zebra Jimnie Gel Rollerball

⭐ Outline each piece with black as shown
✳ This paper is available by the sheet

pattern by Annie Lang
pieced by Paris Dukes

COWBOY BOOT

- patterned Paper Pizazz™: brown sponged (*Mixing Masculine Papers*), barnwood*
- specialty Paper Pizazz™: metallic gold* (*Metallic Gold*)
- solid Paper Pizazz™: black (*Solid Jewel Tones*)
- gold star brad: Magic Scraps™
- black pen: Zebra Jimnie Gel Rollerball

⭐ Mat each piece on black as shown
✳ This paper is available by the sheet

pattern by Jacie Pete
pieced by Paris Dukes

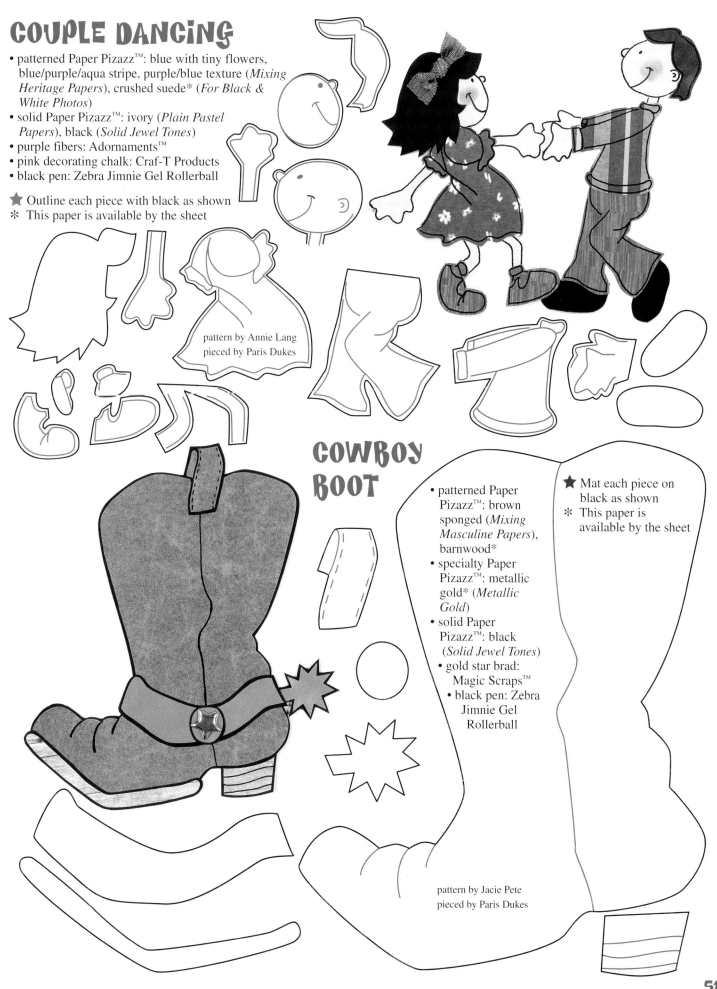

51

COYOTE

- patterned Paper Pizazz™: tan solid, tan embossed, blue embossed, green solid, burgundy embossed (*"Leather" Papers*)
- solid Paper Pizazz™: black (*Solid Jewel Tones*)

★ Mat each piece on black as shown

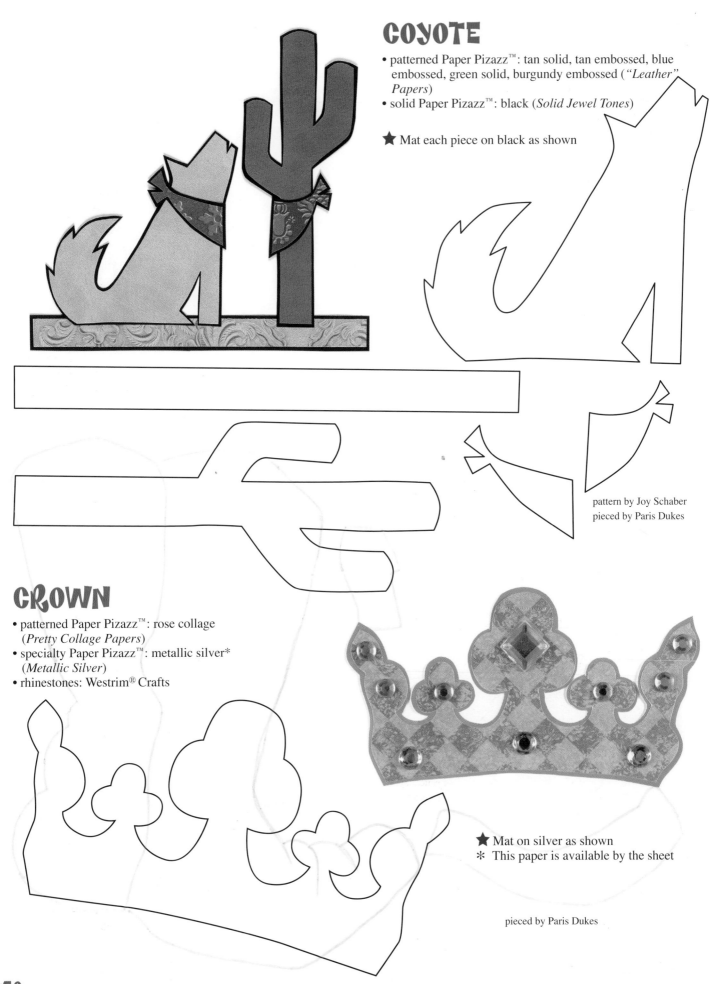

pattern by Joy Schaber
pieced by Paris Dukes

CROWN

- patterned Paper Pizazz™: rose collage (*Pretty Collage Papers*)
- specialty Paper Pizazz™: metallic silver* (*Metallic Silver*)
- rhinestones: Westrim® Crafts

★ Mat on silver as shown
✳ This paper is available by the sheet

pieced by Paris Dukes

CUP CAKE

- patterned Paper Pizazz™: blue with purple dots, purple stripes, purple leaves (*Mixing Soft Patterned Papers*)
- solid Paper Pizazz™: yellow, lavender (*Solid Pastel Papers*), black (*Solid Jewel Tones*)
- yellow, purple, blue seed beads: Blue Moon Beads/ Elizabeth Ward & Co., Inc.

★ Mat each piece on black as shown

pattern by Joy Schaber
pieced by Paris Dukes

DAISY

- patterned Paper Pizazz™: purple/multi-color plaid, yellow with purple floral (*Mixing Soft Patterned Papers*)
- solid Paper Pizazz™: black (*Solid Jewel Tones*)
- black pen: Zig® Writer

★ Mat each piece on black as shown

pattern by Joy Schaber
pieced by Paris Dukes

DIAPER PINS

- patterned Paper Pizazz™: blue gingham* (*Soft Tints*)
- specialty Paper Pizazz™: metallic silver* (*Metallic Silver*)
- solid Paper Pizazz™: black (*Solid Jewel Tones*)
- 24-gauge silver wire: ColourCraft™

★ Mat each piece on black as shown
✳ This paper is available by the sheet

pattern by Annie Lang
pieced by Shauna Berglund-Immel

DOGHOUSE

- patterned Paper Pizazz™: blue squares, blue circles (*Bright Tints*), pet prints*, grass*
- solid Paper Pizazz™: black (*Solid Jewel Tones*), white (*Plain Pastels*)
- bone: Dress It Up
- black pen: Zebra Jimnie Gel Rollerball

★ Mat each piece on black as shown
✳ This paper is available by the sheet

pattern by Joy Schaber
pieced by Paris Dukes

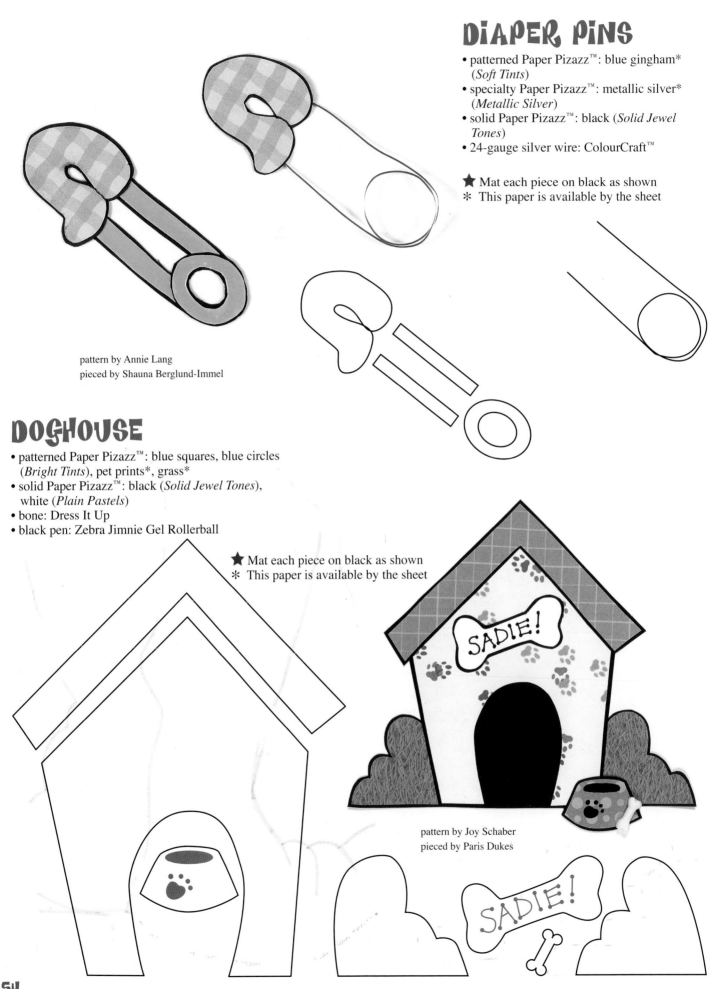

54

EIFFEL TOWER

- patterned Paper Pizazz™: pale green with mosaic, stripe & floral (*Soft Collage Papers*)
- vellum Paper Pizazz™: white* (*Vellum Papers*)
- solid Paper Pizazz™: black (*Solid Jewel Tones*)
- black eyelets: Stamp Studio

★ Mat each piece on black as shown
✳ This paper is available by the sheet

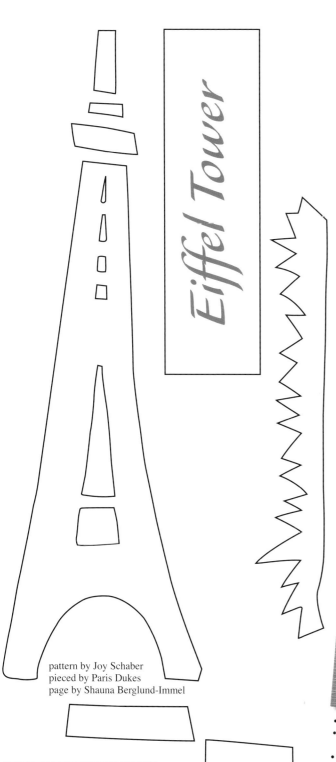

pattern by Joy Schaber
pieced by Paris Dukes
page by Shauna Berglund-Immel

- patterned Paper Pizazz™: green collage (*Pretty Collage Papers*)
- specialty Paper Pizazz™: white vellum (*Vellum Papers*, also by the sheet), metallic silver (*Metallic Silver*, also by the sheet)
- solid Paper Pizazz™: black (*Paper Pizazz™ Solid Jewel Tones*)
- black eyelets, silver fiber: Magic Scraps™

ELEPHANT

- patterned Paper Pizazz™: light blue sponged, pink sponged, tan webbing (*Soft & Subtle Textures*), purple swirls, pink wavy stripes (*Jewel Tints*)
- solid Paper Pizazz™: white (*Plain Pastels*), black (*Solid Jewel Tones*)
- ¼" wide light orchid satin ribbon: C.M Offray & Son, Co.
- pink decorating chalk: Craf-T Prodcuts
- black pen: Zebra Jimnie Gel Rollerball

★ Mat each piece on black as shown

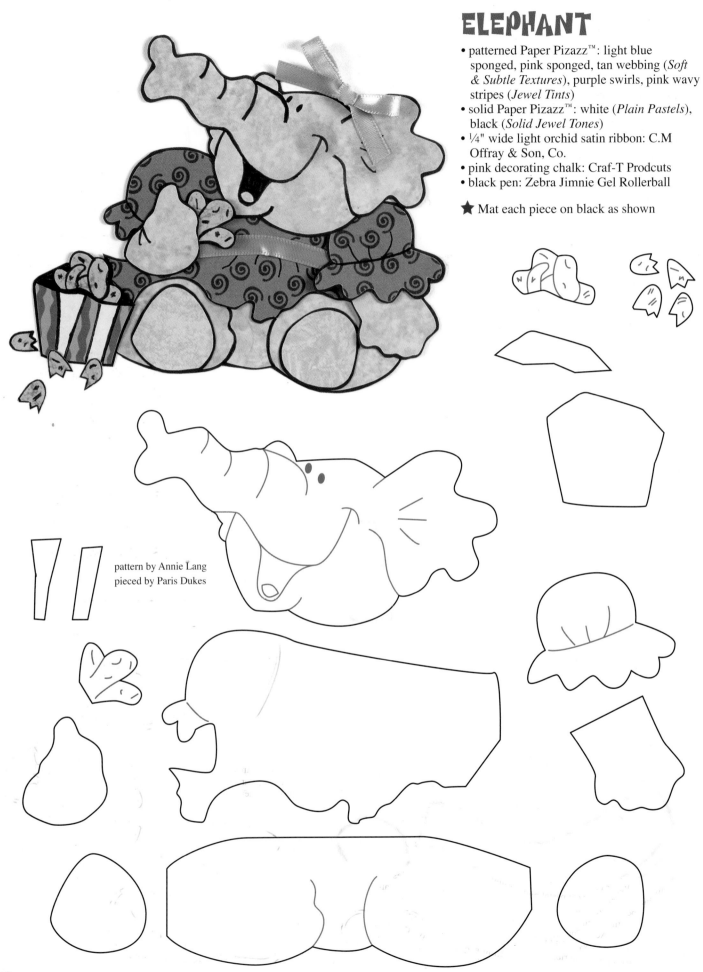

pattern by Annie Lang
pieced by Paris Dukes

ELEPHANTS, MAMA & BABY

- patterned Paper Pizazz™: light blue sponged, tan mosaic, tan webbing (*Soft & Subtle Textures*), yellow/pink posies*, yellow/pink gingham* (*Soft Tints*)
- solid Paper Pizazz™: black (*Solid Jewel Tones*)
- ⅛", ¼" wide pink satin ribbon: C.M. Offray & Son Inc.
- pink decorating chalk: Craf-T Products
- black pen: Zebra Jimnie Gel Rollerball

★ Outline each piece with black as shown
✳ This paper is available by the sheet

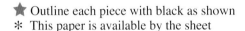

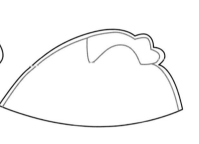

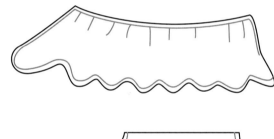

pattern by Annie Lang
pieced by Paris Dukes
page by Arlene Peterson

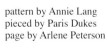

- patterned Paper Pizazz™: yellow/pink gingham, yellow/pink posies (*Soft Tints*)
- specialty Paper Pizazz™: pastel pink vellum (*Pastel Vellum Papers*, also by the sheet)
- solid Paper Pizazz™: white (*Plain Pastels*)
- pink decorating chalks: Craf-T Products
- heart die-cuts: Accu/Cut® Systems
- heart punches: Marvy® Uchida
- ⅛", ¼" wide pink satin ribbon: C.M. Offray & Son

57

EMPIRE STATE BUILDING

- patterned Paper Pizazz™: brown with diamonds, brown sponged (*Mixing Masculine Papers*)
- vellum Paper Pizazz™: ivory*
- solid Paper Pizazz™: black (*Solid Jewel Tones*)
- black eyelets: Stamp Studio
- black pen: Zebra Jimnie Gel Rollerball

★ Mat each piece on black as shown, except vellum

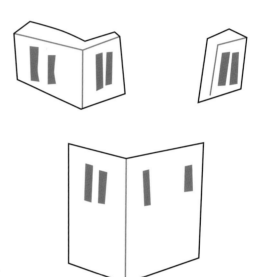

pattern by Joy Schaber
pieced by Paris Dukes

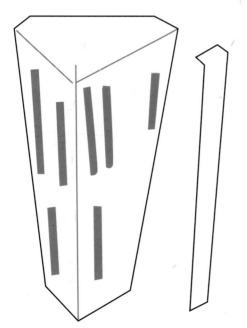

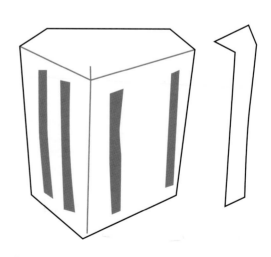

Empire State Building

FIRST PLACE RIBBON

- patterned Paper Pizazz™: blue gingham, blue texture, blue lines/squares (*Mixing Masculine Papers*)
- solid Paper Pizazz™: black (*Solid Jewel Tones*)
- ¼" wide navy blue satin ribbon: C.M. Offray & Son, Inc.
- adhesive foam tape: Therm O Web

★ Mat each piece on black as shown

pattern by Joy Schaber
pieced by Paris Dukes

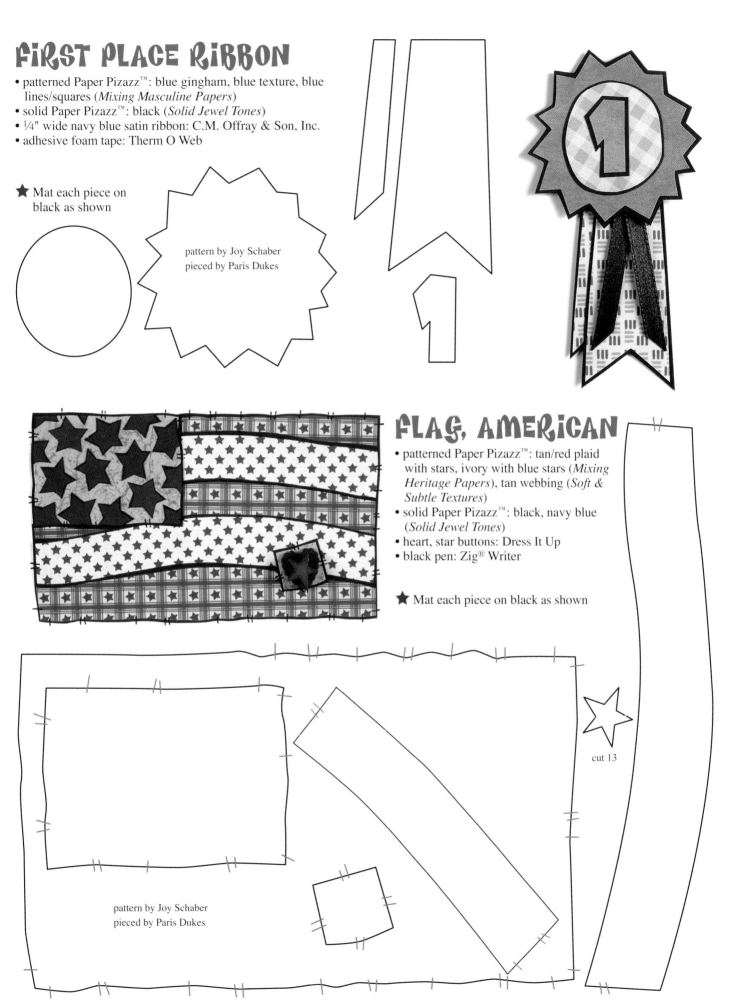

FLAG, AMERICAN

- patterned Paper Pizazz™: tan/red plaid with stars, ivory with blue stars (*Mixing Heritage Papers*), tan webbing (*Soft & Subtle Textures*)
- solid Paper Pizazz™: black, navy blue (*Solid Jewel Tones*)
- heart, star buttons: Dress It Up
- black pen: Zig® Writer

★ Mat each piece on black as shown

cut 13

pattern by Joy Schaber
pieced by Paris Dukes

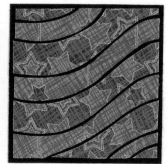
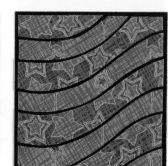

FLAG SQUARES

- patterned Paper Pizazz™: red with blue stars, blue with red stars, red crosshatch (*Mixing Masculine Papers*)
- solid Paper Pizazz™: black, navy blue (*Solid Jewel Tones*)
- heart, star buttons: Dress It Up
- black pen: Zig® Writer

cut 10, or use a star punch

★ Mat each piece on black as shown

cut 3 from blue with red stars, 1 from white

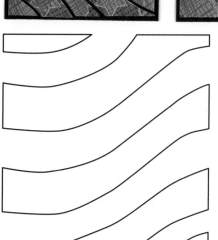
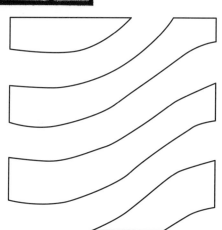
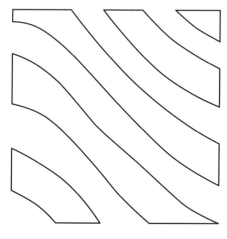

pattern by Jacie Pete
pieced by Paris Dukes

FLIP FLOPS

- patterned Paper Pizazz™: turquoise/burgundy stripe, burgundy sponged (*Mixing Bright Papers*)
- solid Paper Pizazz™: black (*Solid Jewel Tones*)

★ Mat each piece on black as shown

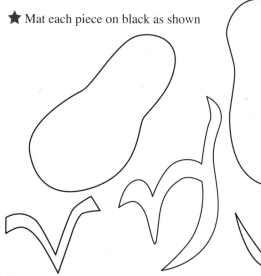

pattern by Joy Schaber
pieced by Paris Dukes

FLOWER

- patterned Paper Pizazz™: turquoise with burgundy flowers, burgundy sponged (*Mixing Bright Papers*)
- solid Paper Pizazz™: black (*Solid Jewel Tones*)
- black seed beads: Blue Moon Beads/Elizabeth Ward & Co., Inc.
- black pen: Zebra Jimnie Gel Rollerball

★ Mat each piece on black as shown

pattern by Joy Schaber
pieced by Paris Dukes

FLOWER POT

- patterned Paper Pizazz™: purple floral, green floral, mauve floral, mauve stripes (*Muted Tints*)
- solid Paper Pizazz™: black (*Solid Jewel Tones*)
- black wire: ColourCraft™
- flower buttons: Dress It Up
- black pen: Zebra Jimnie Gel Rollerball

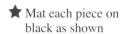

★ Mat each piece on black as shown

pattern by Joy Schaber
pieced by Paris Dukes

FOOTBALL

- patterned Paper Pizazz™: teal circles, brown circles (*Jewel Tints*)
- solid Paper Pizazz™: black (*Solid Jewel Tones*)

★ Mat each piece on black as shown

pattern by Joy Schaber
pieced by Paris Dukes

GECKO

- patterned Paper Pizazz™: green diamonds, brown diamonds (*Jewel Tints*)
- solid Paper Pizazz™: black (*Solid Jewel Tones*)
- black, brown glitter: Magic Scraps™
- black pen: Zebra Jimnie Gel Rollerball

★ Mat each piece on black as shown

pattern by Joy Schaber
pieced by Paris Dukes

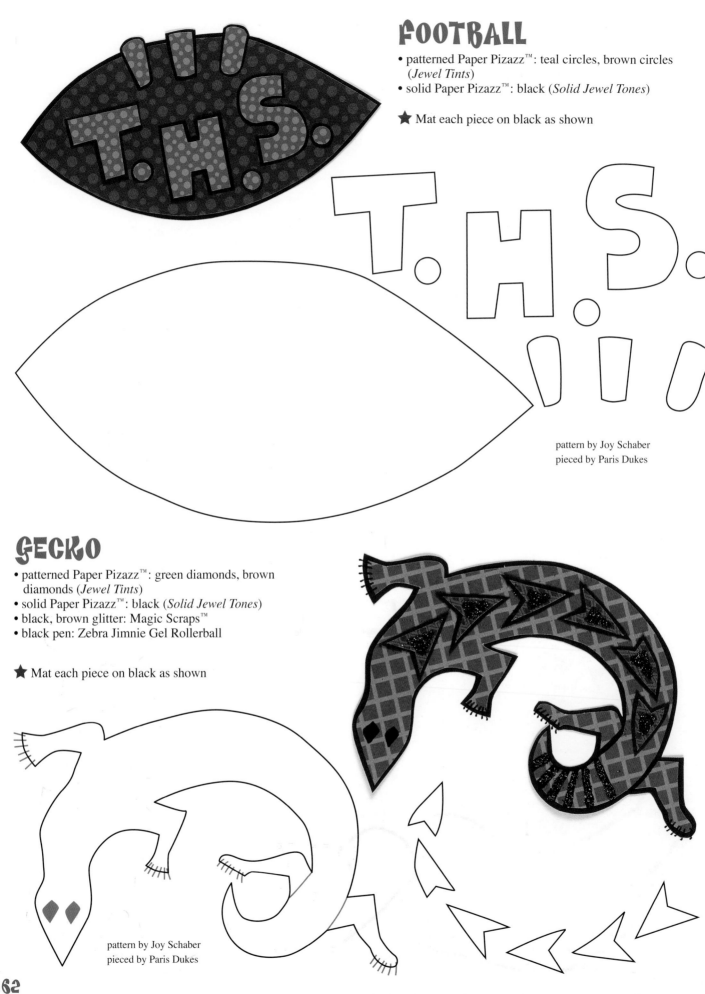

GiRAFFE #1

- patterned Paper Pizazz™: yellow with pink flowers, yellow/pink stripes (*Mixing Light Papers*)
- solid Paper Pizazz™: light pink (*Plain Pastel Papers*), black (*Solid Jewel Tones*)
- gold/yellow fibers: Adornments™
- black pen: Zebra Jimnie Gel Rollerball
- white pen: Milky Lunar Gel Roller
- adhesive foam tape: Therm O Web

★ Mat each piece on black as shown

pattern by Joy Schaber
pieced by Paris Dukes
page by Arlene Peterson

- patterned Paper Pizazz™: yellow with pink flowers, yellow w/pink stripes, pink scuffed with words (*Mixing Light Papers*)
- solid Paper Pizazz™: black (*Paper Pizazz™ Solid Jewel Tones*), pink (*Plain Pastels*)
- yellow fiber: Adornments™
- black eyelets: Magic Scraps™

63

GiRAFFe #2

- patterned Paper Pizazz™: green swirls*, brown swirls*, brown plaid*, clouds*
- solid Paper Pizazz™: black (*Solid Jewel Tones*)
- black pen: Sakura Micron

★ Mat each piece on black as shown
✳ This paper is available by the sheet

pattern by Annie Lang
pieced by Toddi Barclay

GIRL BLOWING BUBBLES

- patterned Paper Pizazz™: yellow/pink gingham*, yellow/pink posies* (*Soft Tints*), tan sponged (*Mixing Light Papers*), black satin (*Mixing Heritage Papers*)
- specialty Paper Pizazz™: white vellum* (*Vellum Papers*)
- solid Paper Pizazz™: light pink, pink, light salmon (*Plain Pastels*)
- pink fiber: Adornments™
- rose decorating chalk: Craf-T Products
- black pen: Zebra Jimmie Gel Rollerball

★ Outline each piece with black as shown
✳ This paper is available by the sheet

pattern by Annie Lang
pieced by Paris Dukes

GIRL WITH PRESENT

★ Mat each piece on black as shown

pattern by Annie Lang
pieced by Shauna Berglund-Immel

- patterned Paper Pizazz™: purple paisley, blue flowers, burgundy floral (*Muted Tints*), gold sponged (*Mixing Light Papers*)
- solid Paper Pizazz™: ivory (*Plain Pastels*), black (*Solid Jewel Tones*)
- peach, red decorating chalks: Craf-T Products
- white, black pens: Sakura Gelly Roll
- salmon pen: Zig® Writer

GIRL WITH TEDDY BEAR

- patterned Paper Pizazz™: purple texture, purple floral, yellow with tiny hearts & stars (*Mixing Baby Papers*)
- solid Paper Pizazz™: black (*Solid Jewel Tones*), pastel yellow, light tan (*Plain Pastels*)
- pink decorating chalk: Craf-T Products
- purple fibers: Adornaments™
- black pen: Zebra Jimnie Gel Rollerball

★ Mat each piece on black as shown

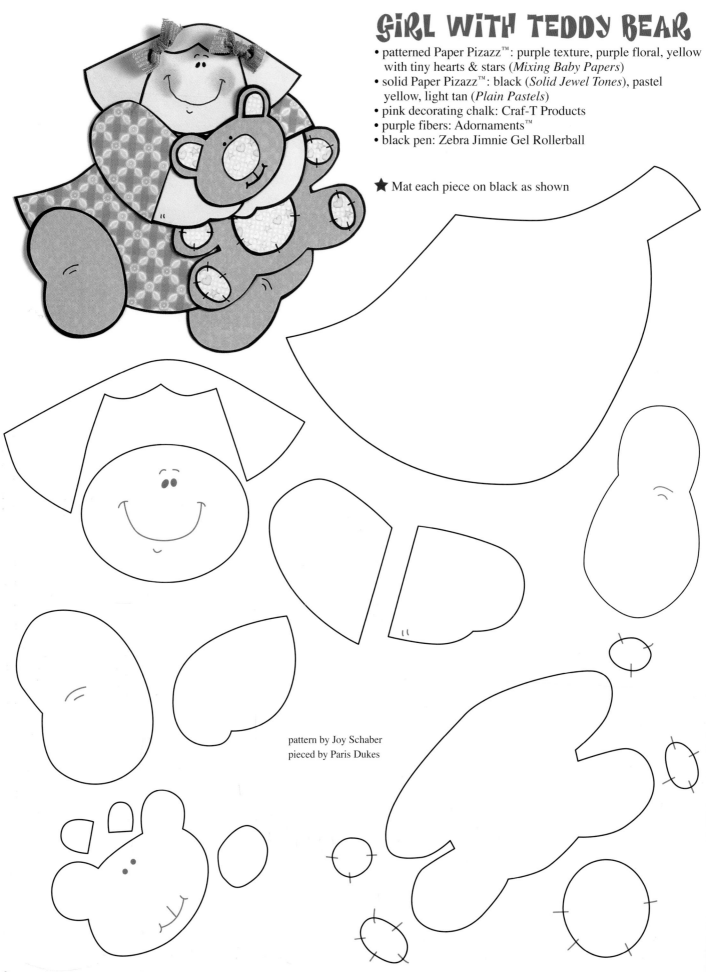

pattern by Joy Schaber
pieced by Paris Dukes

GOLDEN GATE BRIDGE

- patterned Paper Pizazz™: Halloween collage (*Holidays & Seasons Collage*)
- vellum Paper Pizazz™: white* (*Vellum Papers*), pastel blue* (*Pastel Vellum Papers*), ivory*
- solid Paper Pizazz™: black (*Solid Jewel Tones*)
- gray decorating chalk: Craf-T Products
- 24-guage black wire: Artistic Wire Ltd.
- black eyelets: Stamp Studio
- black pen: Zebra Jimnie Gel Rollerball

★ Mat each piece except vellum on black as shown
✳ This paper is available by the sheet

San Francisco

pattern by Joy Schaber
pieced by Paris Dukes

San Francisco

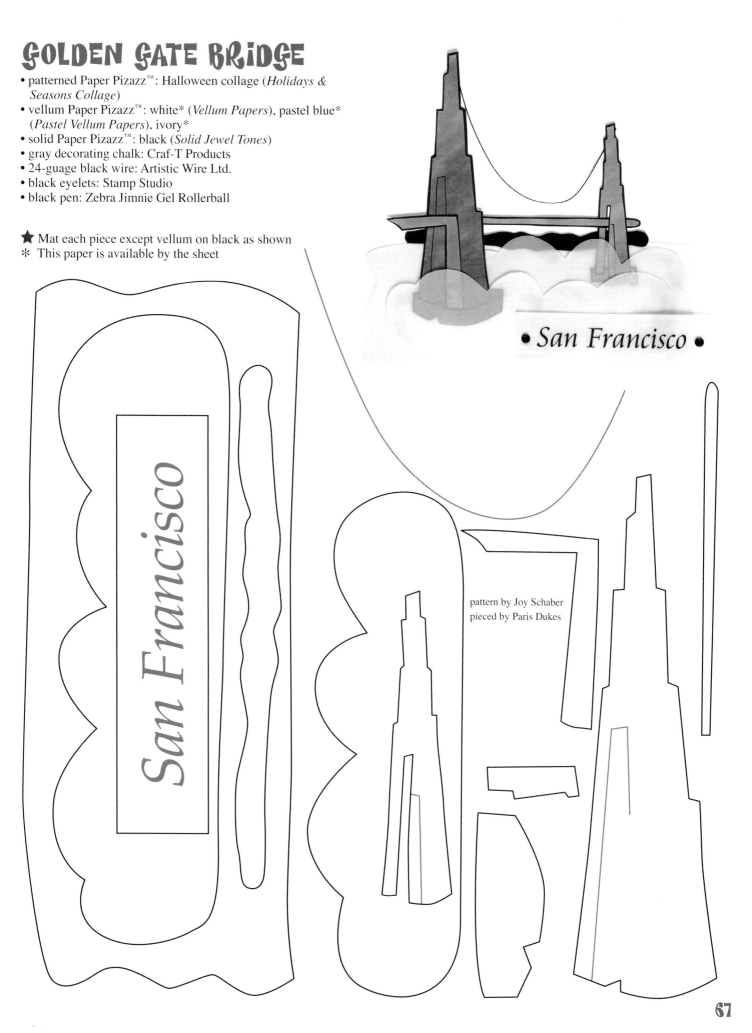

GRANDFATHER CLOCK

- patterned Paper Pizazz™: brown diamond, brown sponged (*Mixing Heritage Papers*)
- specialty Paper Pizazz™: metallic gold* (*Metallic Gold*)
- solid Paper Pizazz™: black (*Solid Jewel Tones*)
- gold clock charm: S. Axelrod Co.

★ Mat each piece on black as shown
✻ This paper is available by the sheet

pattern by Joy Schaber
pieced by Paris Dukes

GUMBALL MACHINE

- patterned Paper Pizazz™: blue square, blue circles, blue swirls*, pink swirls*, yellow swirls* (*Bright Tints*)
- specialty Paper Pizazz™: metallic silver* (*Metallic Silver*), white vellum* (*Vellum Papers*)
- solid Paper Pizazz™: black (*Solid Jewel Tones*)

cut 15,
or use a circle punch

★ Mat each piece on black as shown, except vellum
✻ This paper is available by the sheet

pattern by Jacie Pete
pieced by Paris Dukes

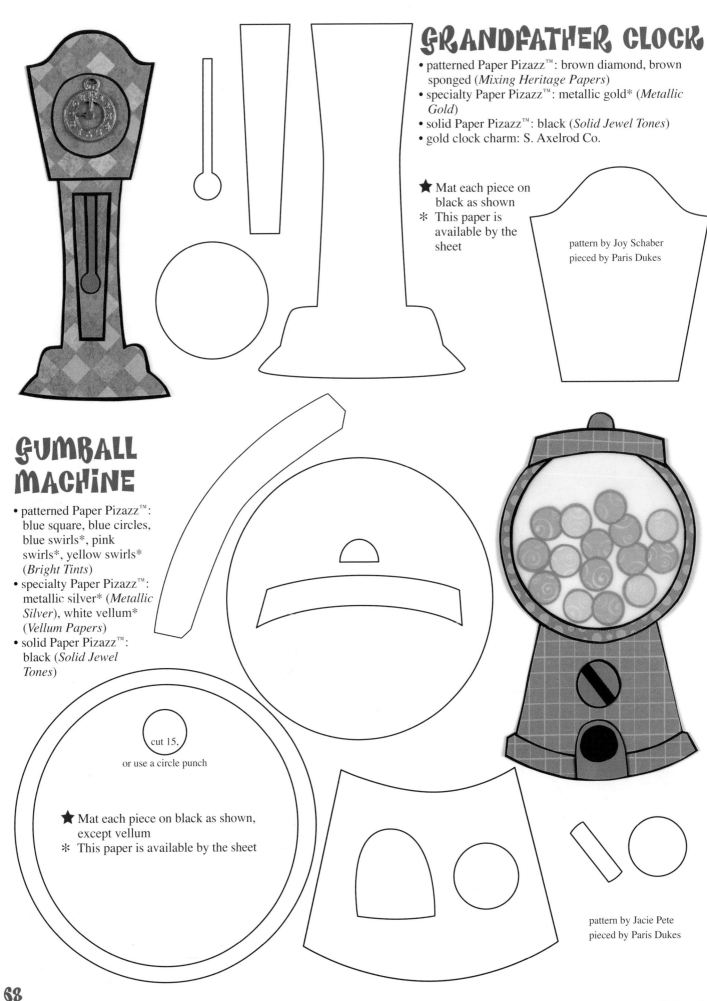

HARD HAT

- specialty Paper Pizazz™: metallic silver* (*Metallic Silver*)
- solid Paper Pizazz™: black (*Solid Jewel Tones*)
- silver eyelets: Stamp Studio

★ Mat each piece on black as shown
✳ This paper is available by the sheet

pattern by Joy Schaber
pieced by Paris Dukes

HARP

- specialty Paper Pizazz™: metallic gold* (*Metallic Gold*)
- solid Paper Pizazz™: black (*Solid Jewel Tones*)
- gold music charm: S. Axelrod Co.
- gold embroidery floss: DMC
- black pen: Zebra Jimnie Gel Rollerball

pattern by Joy Schaber
pieced by Paris Dukes

★ Mat each piece on black as shown
✳ This paper is available by the sheet

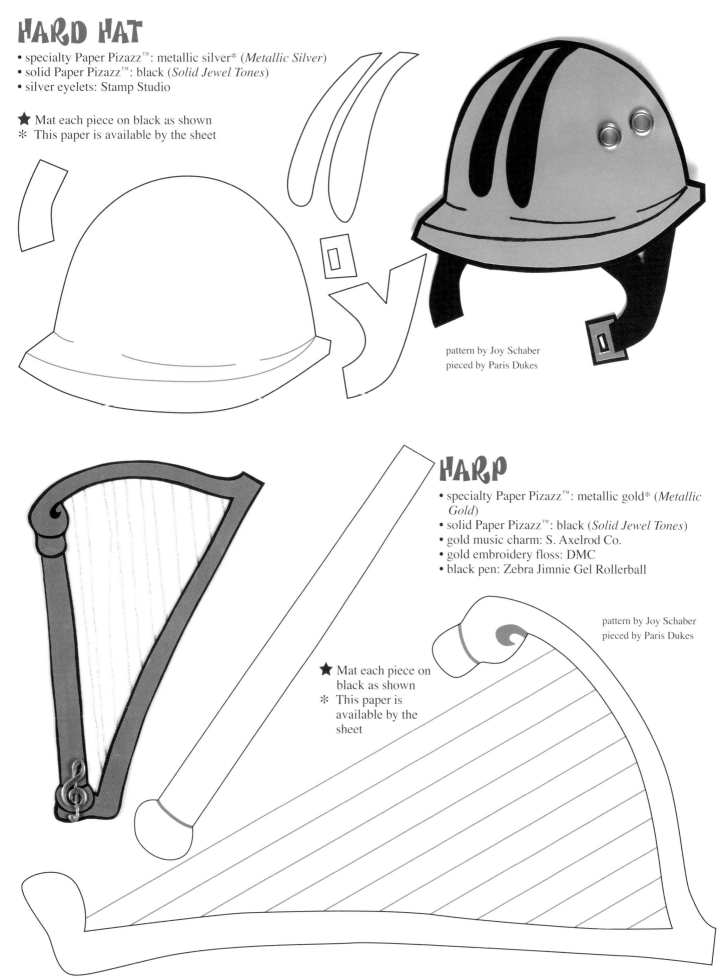

69

HAT, CAPTAIN'S

- patterned Paper Pizazz™: white with blue stars (*Mixing Heritage Papers*)
- specialty Paper Pizazz™: metallic silver* (*Metallic Silver*)
- solid Paper Pizazz™: navy blue, black (*Solid Jewel Tones*)
- silver star tack: Making Memories™

★ Mat each piece on black as shown
✳ This paper is available by the sheet

pattern by Joy Schaber
piece by Paris Dukes

HAT, CHEF'S

- patterned Paper Pizazz™: yellow dots*, yellow stripes* (*Soft Tints*)
- solid Paper Pizazz™: black (*Solid Jewel Tones*)
- alphabet beads: Darice, Inc.
- adhesive foam tape: Therm O Web

★ Mat each piece on black as shown
✳ This paper is available by the sheet

pattern by Joy Schaber
piece by Paris Dukes

HAT, LADY'S

- patterned Paper Pizazz™: tan collage words (*Masculine Collage Papers*)
- solid Paper Pizazz™: black (*Solid Jewel Tones*), tan (*Solid Pastel Papers*)
- ¼" wide ivory ribbon, 1" brown ribbon flower: C.M. Offray & Son, Inc.
- black pen: Zebra Jimmie Gel Rollerball
- adhesive foam tape: Therm O Web

pattern by Joy Schaber
piece by Paris Dukes

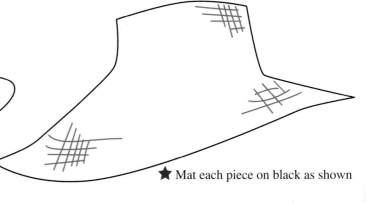

★ Mat each piece on black as shown

HAT, SPANISH

- patterned Paper Pizazz™: brown diamonds, brown dots (*Jewel Tints*)
- solid Paper Pizazz™: black (*Solid Jewel Tones*)
- multi-colored fibers: Adornaments™
- silver metal beads: Blue Moon Beads/Elizabeth Ward & Co., Inc.

★ Mat each piece on black as shown

pattern by Joy Schaber
pieced by Paris Dukes

HEART FLAG

- patterned Paper Pizazz™: tan/red plaid with stars, ivory with blue stars (*Mixing Heritage Papers*), tan webbing (*Soft & Subtle Textures*), denim*
- solid Paper Pizazz™: black (*Solid Jewel Tones*)
- star button: Dress It Up
- black pen: Zebra Jimnie Gel Rollerball

★ Mat each piece on black as shown
✳ This paper is available by the sheet

pattern by Joy Schaber
pieced by Paris Dukes

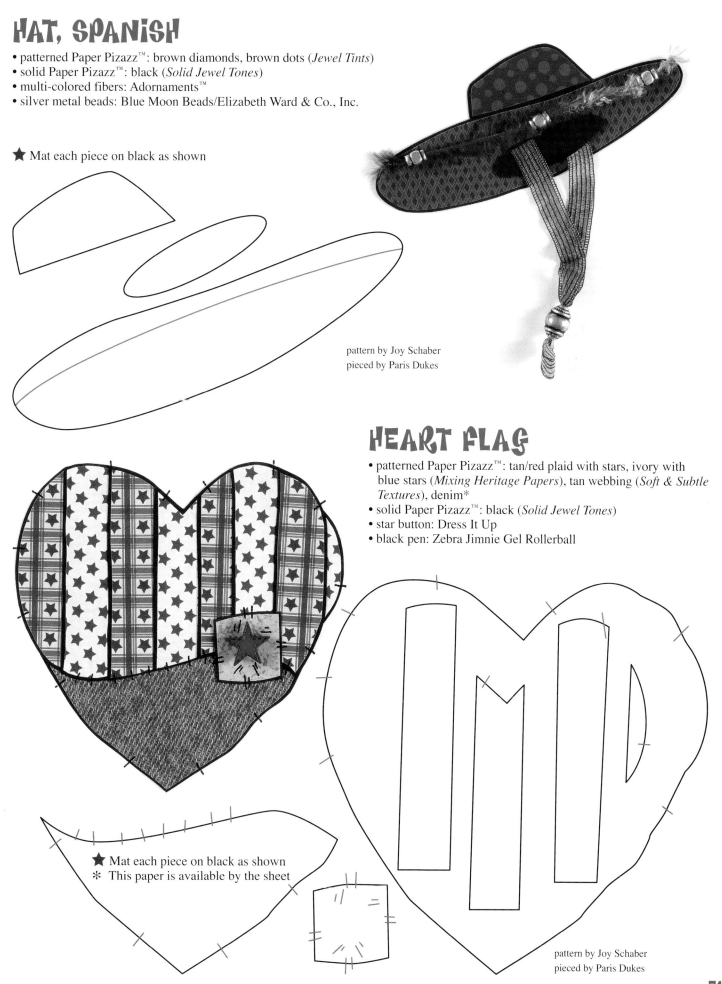

HORSE HEAD

- patterned Paper Pizazz™: tan*, brown (*Flowered "Handmade" Papers*)
- solid Paper Pizazz™: black (*Solid Jewel Tones*)
- white pen: Pentel Milky Lunar Gel Roller
- black pen: Zebra Jimmie Gel Rollerball

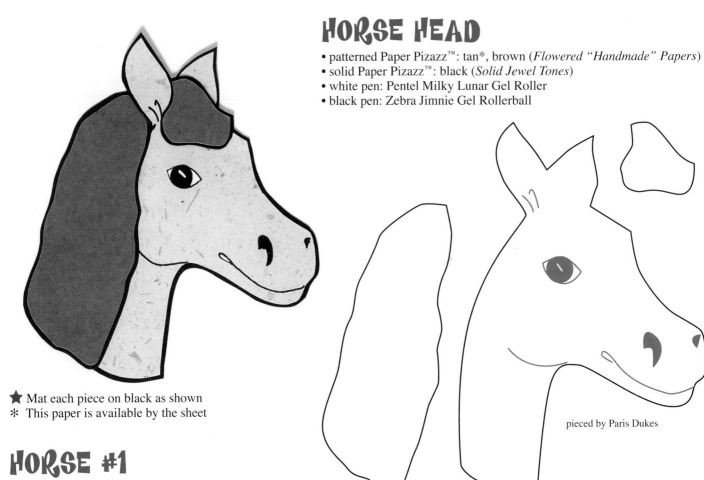

★ Mat each piece on black as shown
✴ This paper is available by the sheet

pieced by Paris Dukes

HORSE #1

- patterned Paper Pizazz™: ivory roses*, crushed suede*
  (*For Black & White Photos*)
- solid Paper Pizazz™: black (*Solid Jewel Tones*)
- black pen: Zebra Jimmie Gel Rollerball

★ Mat each piece on black as shown
✴ This paper is available by the sheet

pattern by Joy Schaber
pieced by Paris Dukes

HORSE #2

- patterned Paper Pizazz™: pink crackle, pink sponged (*Soft & Subtle Textures*)
- solid Paper Pizazz™: black (*Solid Jewel Tones*), white (*Plain Pastels*)
- shaved ice glitter: Magic Scraps™
- black pen: Zebra Jimnie Gel Rollerball

★ Mat each piece on black as shown

pattern by Joy Schaber
pieced by Paris Dukes

HORSE #3

- patterned Paper Pizazz™: gray with rhinos (*Wild Things*)
- solid Paper Pizazz™: black (*Solid Jewel Tones*)
- black fibers: Magic Scraps™
- black pen: Zebra Jimnie Gel Rollerball

★ Mat each piece on black as shown

pattern by Joy Schaber
pieced by Paris Dukes

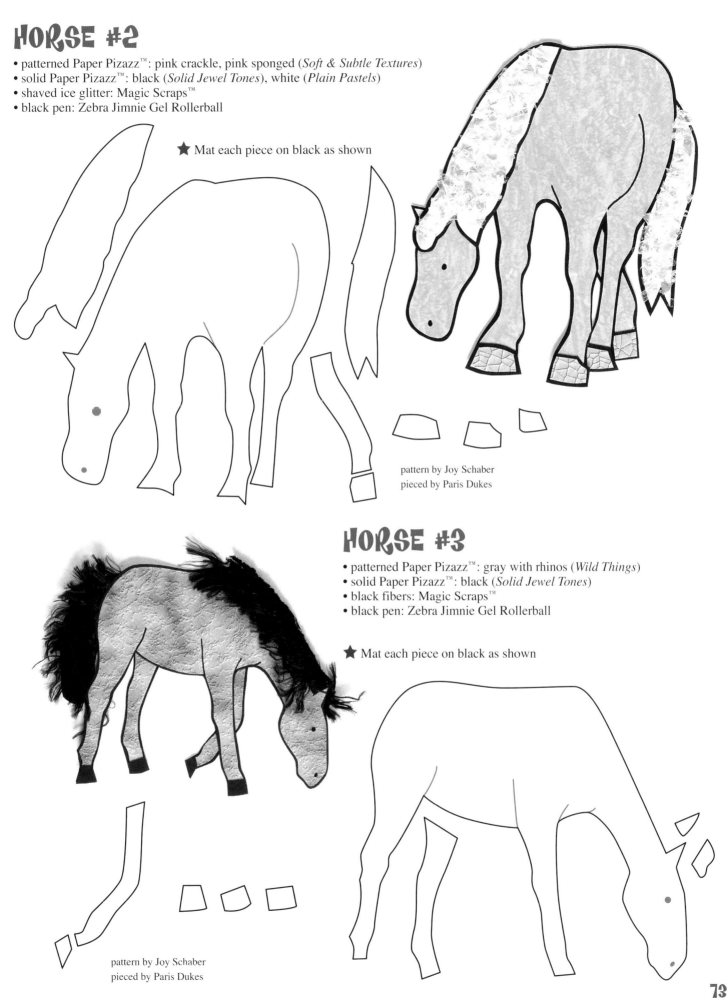

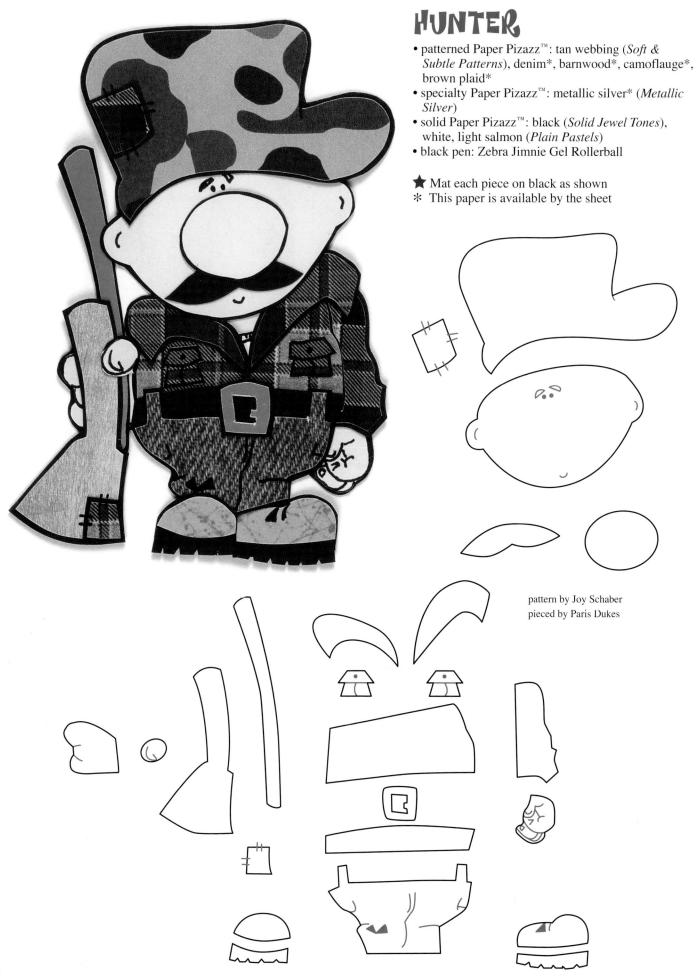

HUNTER

- patterned Paper Pizazz™: tan webbing (*Soft & Subtle Patterns*), denim*, barnwood*, camoflauge*, brown plaid*
- specialty Paper Pizazz™: metallic silver* (*Metallic Silver*)
- solid Paper Pizazz™: black (*Solid Jewel Tones*), white, light salmon (*Plain Pastels*)
- black pen: Zebra Jimnie Gel Rollerball

★ Mat each piece on black as shown
✳ This paper is available by the sheet

pattern by Joy Schaber
pieced by Paris Dukes

IRIS

- patterned Paper Pizazz™: light blue paisley, light purple paisley, green floral (*12"x12" Muted Tints*)
- solid Paper Pizazz™: black (*Solid Jewel Tones*)
- seed beads: Blue Moon Beads/Elizabeth Ward & Co., Inc.
- ⅝" wide sheer lavender ribbon: Sheer Creations
- black pen: Zebra Jimnie Gel Rollerball
- adhesive foam tape: Therm O Web

★ Mat each piece on black as shown
✳ This paper is available by the sheet

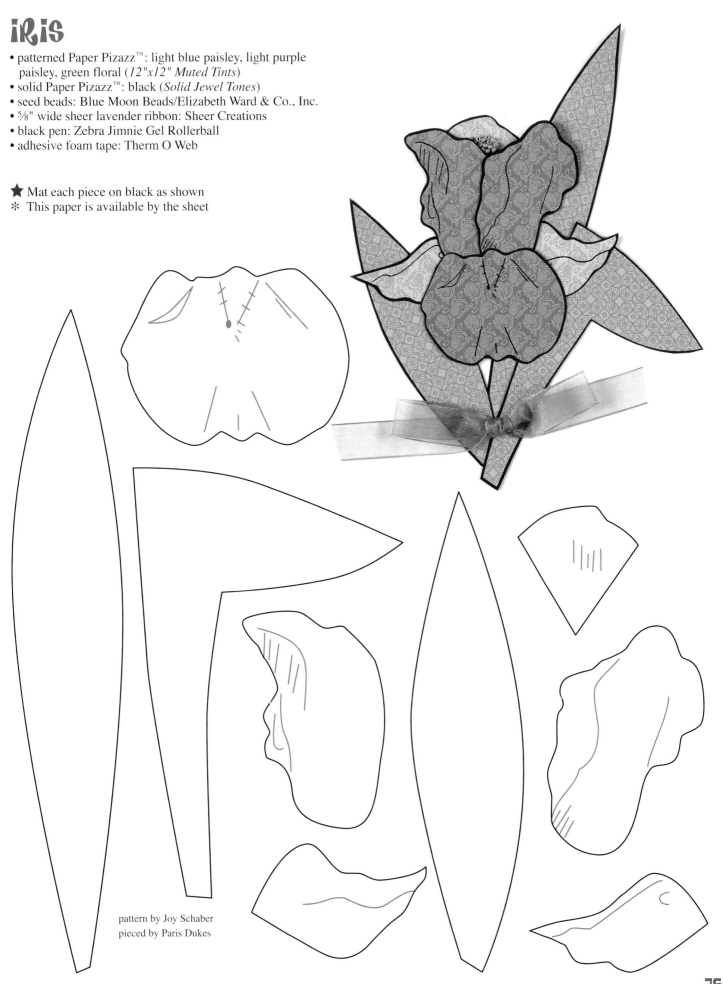

pattern by Joy Schaber
pieced by Paris Dukes

IVY

- patterned Paper Pizazz™: green floral (*Muted Tints*)
- solid Paper Pizazz™: black (*Solid Jewel Tones*)
- 24-guage black wire: Artistic Wire Ltd.
- black pen: Zebra Jimnie Gel Rollerball

★ Mat each piece on black as shown

pattern by Jacie Pete
pieced by Paris Dukes

KARATE

- patterned Paper Pizazz™: gray with border, black with dots (*Heritage Papers*)
- solid Paper Pizazz™: black (*Solid Jewel Tones*), pastel yellow (*Plain Pastels*)
- black pen: Zebra Jimnie Gel Rollerball

★ Mat each piece on black as shown

cut 2

cut 2

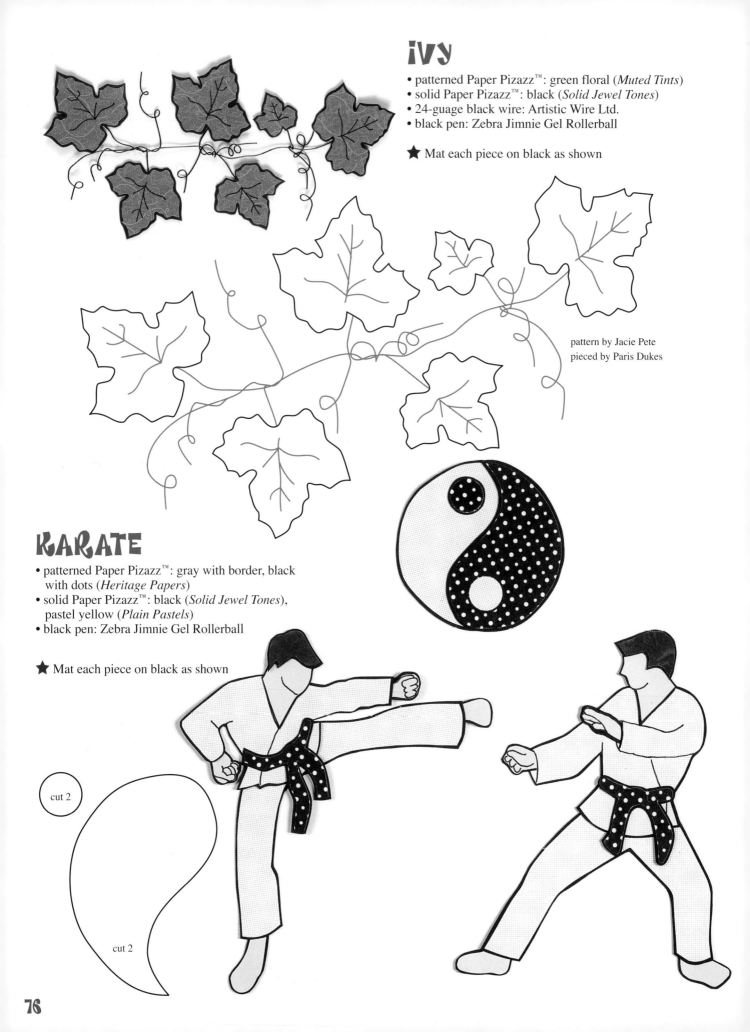

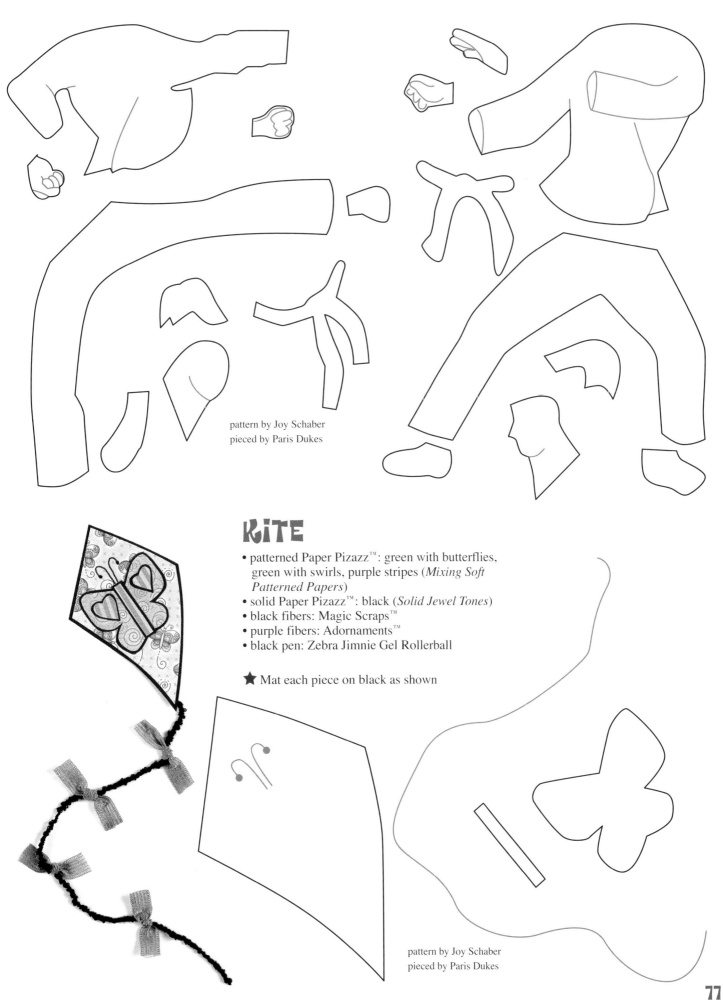

pattern by Joy Schaber
pieced by Paris Dukes

KITE

- patterned Paper Pizazz™: green with butterflies, green with swirls, purple stripes (*Mixing Soft Patterned Papers*)
- solid Paper Pizazz™: black (*Solid Jewel Tones*)
- black fibers: Magic Scraps™
- purple fibers: Adornaments™
- black pen: Zebra Jimnie Gel Rollerball

★ Mat each piece on black as shown

pattern by Joy Schaber
pieced by Paris Dukes

KITTEN

- patterned Paper Pizazz™: yellow stripe,* yellow gingham,* pink posies* (*Soft Tints*)
- specialty Paper Pizazz™: metallic silver* (*Metallic Silver*)
- solid Paper Pizazz™: black (*Solid Jewel Tones*)
- black pen: Zebra Jimnie Gel Rollerball

★ Mat each piece on black as shown
✳ This paper is available by the sheet

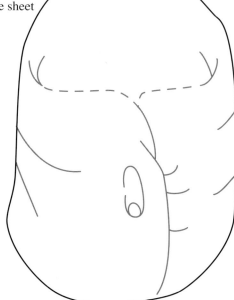

pattern by Annie Lang
pieced by Shauna Berglund-Immel

LADY BUG

- patterned Paper Pizazz™: red sponged (*Mixing Bright Papers*)
- solid Paper Pizazz™: black (*Solid Jewel Tones*)
- black, white, red decorating chalks: Craf-T Products
- white, black pens: Sakura Gelly Roll

pattern by Annie Lang
pieced by Shauna Berglund-Immel

★ Mat select pieces on black as shown

LEANING TOWER OF PISA

- patterned Paper Pizazz™: grass*, crackle*
- vellum Paper Pizazz™: ivory*
- solid Paper Pizazz™: black (*Solid Jewel Tones*)
- black eyelets: Stamp Studio

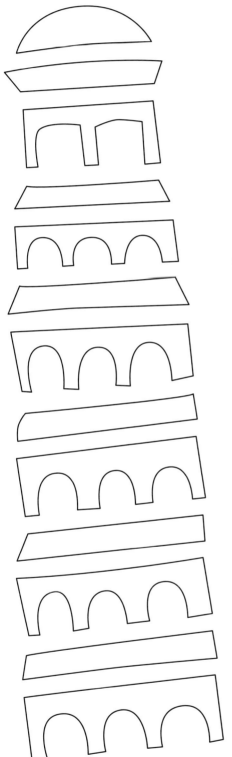

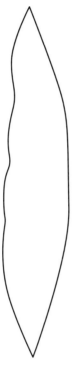

★ Mat each piece on black as shown, except vellum
* This paper is available by the sheet

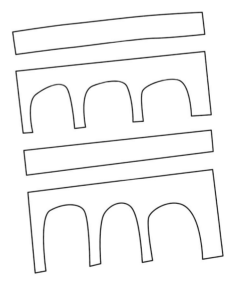

pieced by Paris Dukes

LEANING TOWER OF PISA

LIFE PRESERVER

- solid Paper Pizazz™: black (*Solid Jewel Tones*), red (*Plain Brights*), white (*Plain Pastels*)
- hemp twine: Darice

★ Mat each piece on black as shown

pattern by Annie Lang
pieced by Shauna Berglund-Immel

LIGHT HOUSE

- patterned Paper Pizazz™: cruise ship (*Vacation Collage*)
- vellum Paper Pizazz™: pastel blue* (*Pastel Vellum Papers*)
- solid Paper Pizazz™: black (*Solid Jewel Tones*)
- black pen: Zebra Jimnie Gel Rollerball

★ Mat each piece on black as shown, except vellum
★ Outline vellum piece with black as shown
* This paper is available by the sheet

pattern by Joy Schaber
pieced by Paris Dukes

LILIES

- patterned Paper Pizazz™: green floral, pink with mauve floral, mauve with pink floral, blue paisley (*Muted Tints*)
- seed beads: Blue Moon Bead/Elizabeth Ward & Co., Inc.
- black pen: Zebra Jimnie Gel Rollerball

⭐ Outline each piece with black as shown

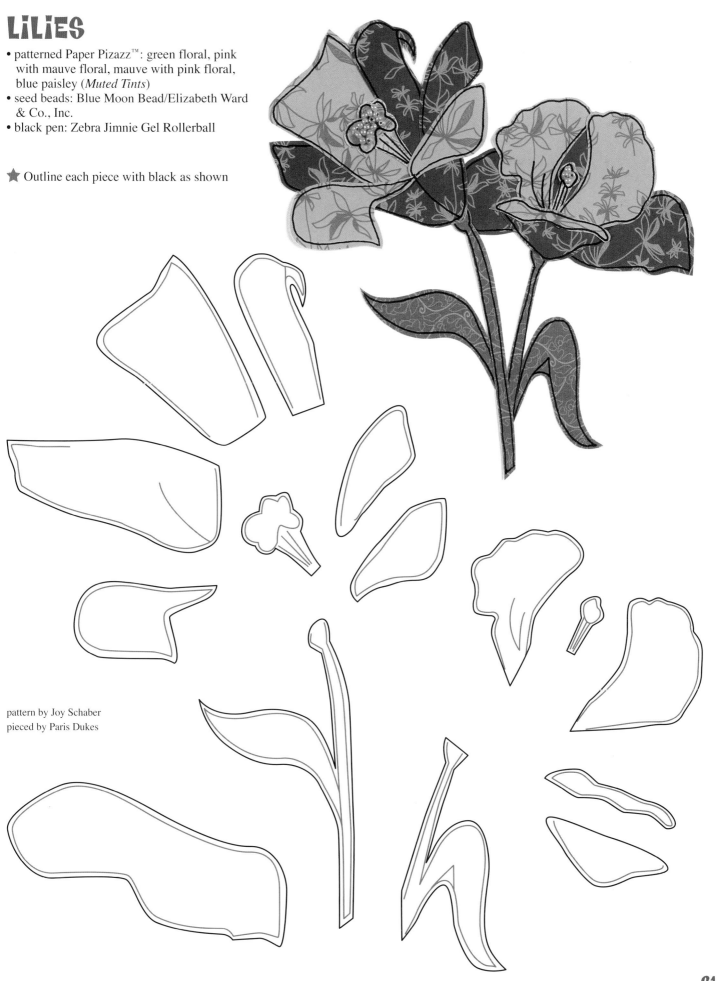

pattern by Joy Schaber
pieced by Paris Dukes

LION #1

- patterned Paper Pizazz™: tan sponge, tan plaid with peach dots (*Mixing Light Papers*)
- solid Paper Pizazz™: black (*Solid Jewel Tones*)
- fibers: Adornaments™
- white pen: Milky Lunar Gel Roller
- black pen: Zebra Jimnie Gel Rollerball
- adhesive foam tape: Therm O Web

★ Mat each piece on black as shown
✳ This paper is available by the sheet

cut 2

pattern by Joy Schaber
pieced by Paris Dukes

LION #2

- patterned Paper Pizazz™: beige spattered, blue sponged with stars (*Spattered, Crackled, Sponged*)
- solid Paper Pizazz™: black (*Solid Jewel Tones*)
- brown Twistel™: Making Memories™
- white, black pens: Sakura Gelly Roll
- adhesive foam tape: Therm O Web

pattern by Annie Lang
pieced by Shauna Berglund-Immel

★ Mat each lion piece on black, mat diamond on gold then black as shown

LION & LAMB

- patterned Paper Pizazz™: yellow with dots, yellow with hearts, white with yellow dots, white with yellow speckles (*Lisa Williams Blue, Yellow & Green*)
- solid Paper Pizazz™: black (*Solid Jewel Tones*)
- yellow fibers: Adornaments™
- pom poms: Westrim® Crafts
- black pen: Zebra Jimnie Gel Rollerball
- adhesive foam tape: Therm O Web

★ Mat each piece on black as shown

pattern by Joy Schaber
pieced by Paris Dukes

LOG CABIN

- patterned Paper Pizazz™: brown sponged/solid, green/brown stripes, green pinecone/pine sprig (*Mixing Masculine Papers*)
- vellum Paper Pizazz™: white* (*Vellum Papers*)
- solid Paper Pizazz™: black (*Solid Jewel Tones*)
- black pen: Zebra Jimnie Gel Rollerball

★ Mat each piece on black as shown

pattern by Joy Schaber
pieced by Paris Dukes

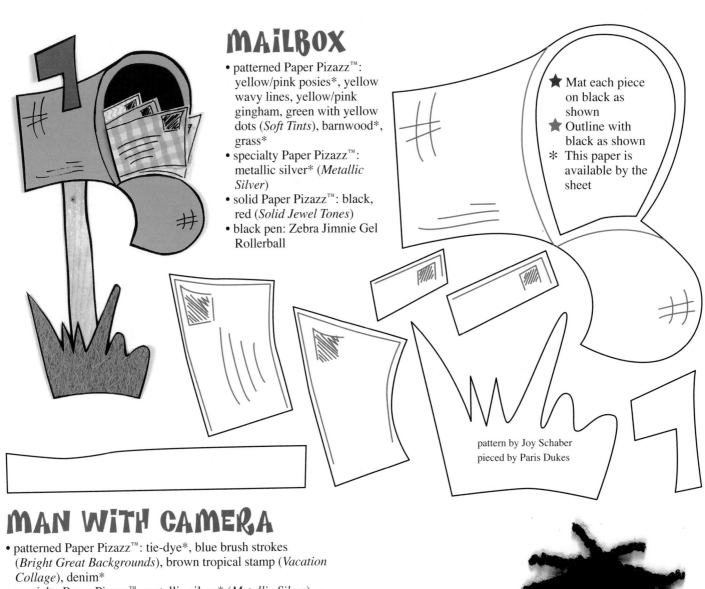

MAILBOX

- patterned Paper Pizazz™: yellow/pink posies*, yellow wavy lines, yellow/pink gingham, green with yellow dots (*Soft Tints*), barnwood*, grass*
- specialty Paper Pizazz™: metallic silver* (*Metallic Silver*)
- solid Paper Pizazz™: black, red (*Solid Jewel Tones*)
- black pen: Zebra Jimnie Gel Rollerball

★ Mat each piece on black as shown
★ Outline with black as shown
* This paper is available by the sheet

pattern by Joy Schaber
pieced by Paris Dukes

MAN WITH CAMERA

- patterned Paper Pizazz™: tie-dye*, blue brush strokes (*Bright Great Backgrounds*), brown tropical stamp (*Vacation Collage*), denim*
- specialty Paper Pizazz™: metallic silver* (*Metallic Silver*)
- solid Paper Pizazz™: light salmon (*Plain Pastels*)
- black fibers: Adornaments™
- buttons: Magic Scraps™
- black pen: Zebra Jimnie Gel Rollerball

★ Outline each piece with black as shown
* This paper is available by the sheet

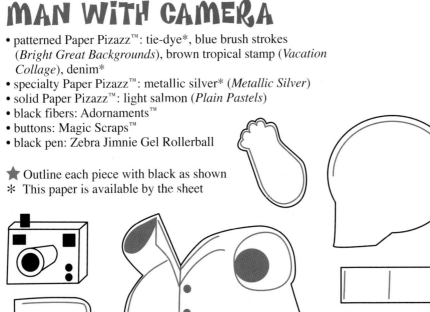

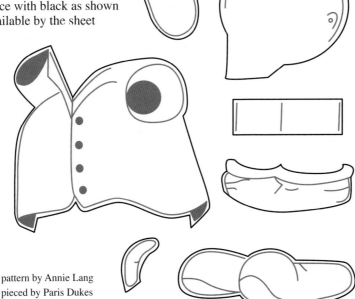

pattern by Annie Lang
pieced by Paris Dukes

MEGAPHONE

- patterned Paper Pizazz™: yellow diamonds (*Soft Tints*)
- solid Paper Pizazz™: black (*Solid Jewel Tones*)
- black glitter: Magic Scraps™
- black pen: Zig® Writer

pattern by Joy Schaber
pieced by Paris Dukes

★ Mat each piece on black as shown

MONKEY #1

- patterned Paper Pizazz™: purple plaid, brown texture, brown stars, gray plaid, green leaves (*Mixing Masculine Papers*)
- solid Paper Pizazz™: black (*Solid Jewel Tones*)
- black pen: Sakura Micron

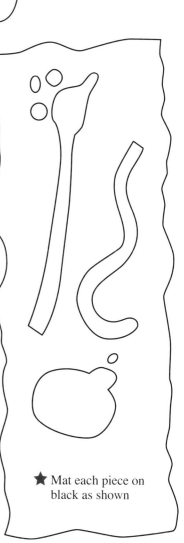

★ Mat each piece on black as shown

pattern by Annie Lang
pieced by Toddi Barclay

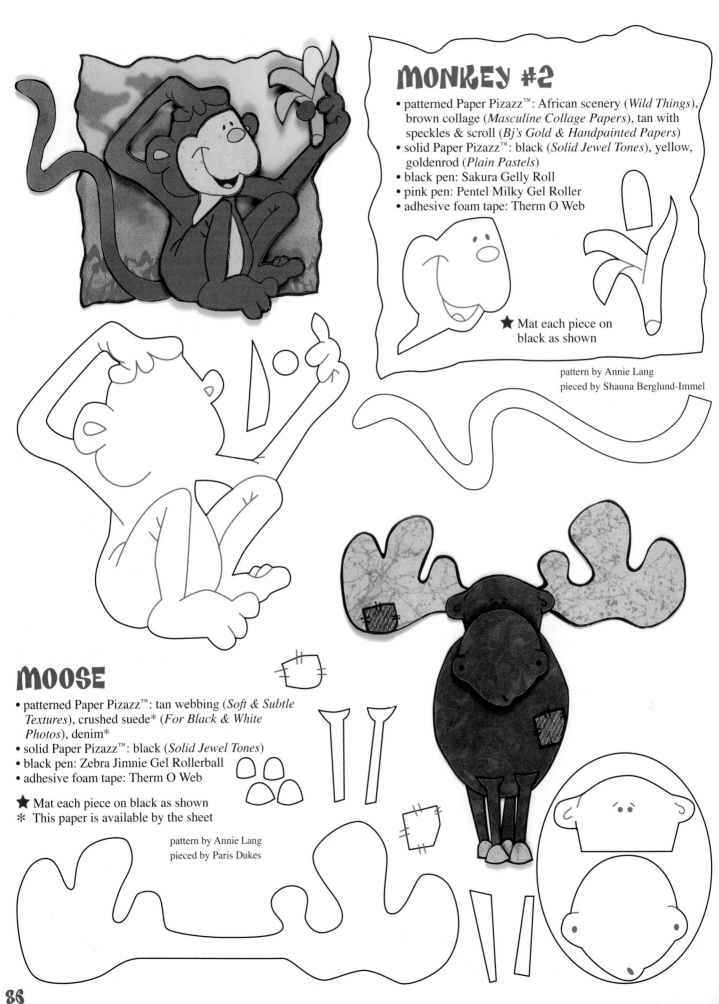

MONKEY #2

- patterned Paper Pizazz™: African scenery (*Wild Things*), brown collage (*Masculine Collage Papers*), tan with speckles & scroll (*Bj's Gold & Handpainted Papers*)
- solid Paper Pizazz™: black (*Solid Jewel Tones*), yellow, goldenrod (*Plain Pastels*)
- black pen: Sakura Gelly Roll
- pink pen: Pentel Milky Gel Roller
- adhesive foam tape: Therm O Web

★ Mat each piece on black as shown

pattern by Annie Lang
pieced by Shauna Berglund-Immel

MOOSE

- patterned Paper Pizazz™: tan webbing (*Soft & Subtle Textures*), crushed suede* (*For Black & White Photos*), denim*
- solid Paper Pizazz™: black (*Solid Jewel Tones*)
- black pen: Zebra Jimnie Gel Rollerball
- adhesive foam tape: Therm O Web

★ Mat each piece on black as shown
✳ This paper is available by the sheet

pattern by Annie Lang
pieced by Paris Dukes

MORTARBOARD & DIPLOMA

- patterned Paper Pizazz™: blue/pink daisies on black (*Mixing Jewel Patterned Papers*), blue/pink (*The Handmade Look*)
- solid Paper Pizazz™: black (*Solid Jewel Tones*), white (*Plain Pastels*)
- pink fibers: Adornaments™
- pink tassle: The Card Connection™
- pink flower eyelet: Making Memories™
- white pen: Sanford Uniball Gel
- black pen: Zebra Jimnie Gel Rollerball
- adhesive foam tape: Therm O Web

you go girl!

you go girl!

★ Mat the diploma and the tag on black as shown

pieced by Paris Dukes

MOUSE

- patterned Paper Pizazz™: gold sponged, blue with yellow dots (*Mixing Light Papers*)
- solid Paper Pizazz™: black (*Solid Jewel Tones*)
- ¼" wide light blue satin ribbon: C.M. Offray & Son, Inc.
- black heart bead: Blue Moon Beads/Elizabeth Ward & Co., Inc.
- 24-gauge black wire: ColourCraft™
- pink decorating chalk: Craf-T Products
- black, white pens: Sakura Gelly Roll

pattern by Annie Lang
pieced by Shauna Berglund-Immel

★ Mat each piece on black as shown

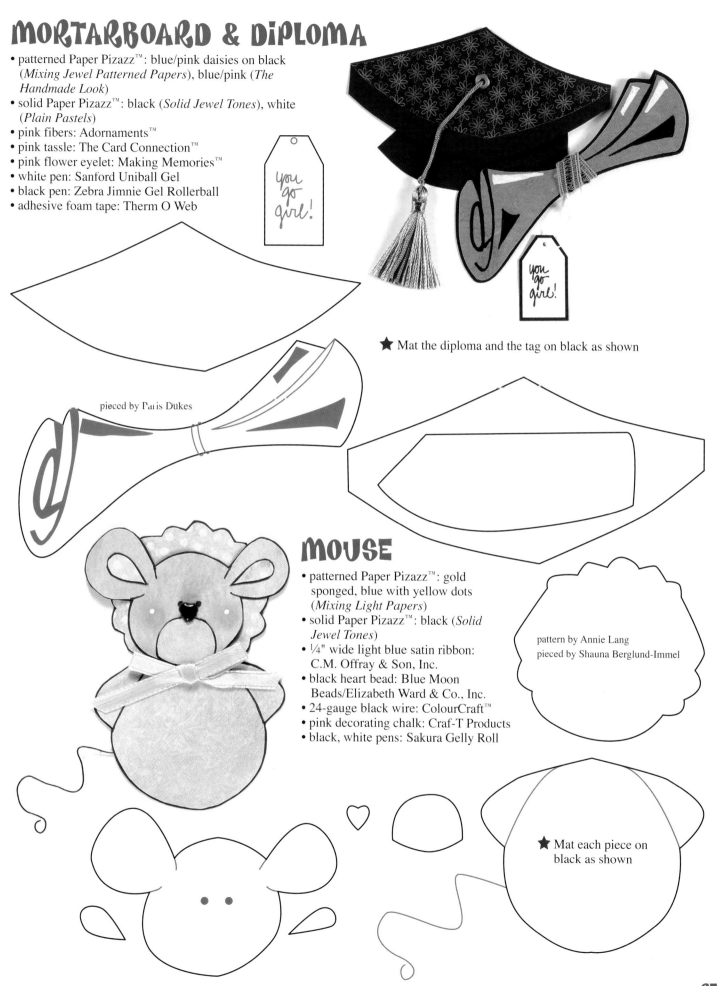

87

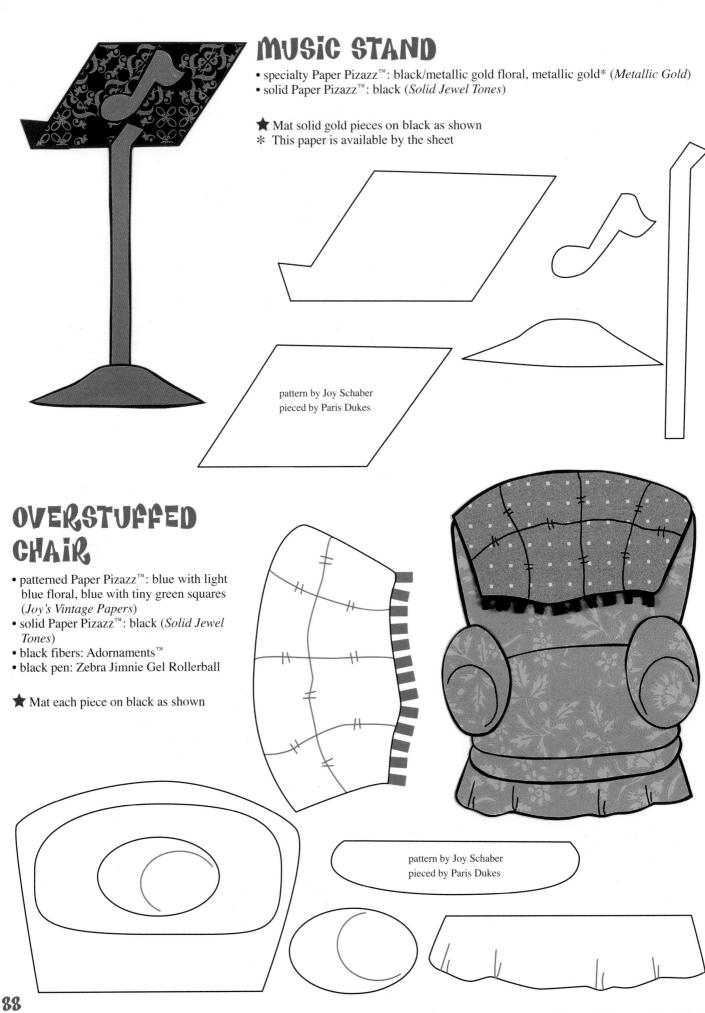

MUSIC STAND

- specialty Paper Pizazz™: black/metallic gold floral, metallic gold* (*Metallic Gold*)
- solid Paper Pizazz™: black (*Solid Jewel Tones*)

★ Mat solid gold pieces on black as shown
✳ This paper is available by the sheet

pattern by Joy Schaber
pieced by Paris Dukes

OVERSTUFFED CHAIR

- patterned Paper Pizazz™: blue with light blue floral, blue with tiny green squares (*Joy's Vintage Papers*)
- solid Paper Pizazz™: black (*Solid Jewel Tones*)
- black fibers: Adornaments™
- black pen: Zebra Jimnie Gel Rollerball

★ Mat each piece on black as shown

pattern by Joy Schaber
pieced by Paris Dukes

PALM TREES

- patterned Paper Pizazz™: brown diamonds, green zig-zag, green wavy stripes, purple triangles (*Jewel Tints*)
- solid Paper Pizazz™: black (*Solid Jewel Tones*)
- brown glitter: Magic Scraps™
- black pen: Zebra Jimnie Gel Rollerball

★ Mat each piece on black as shown

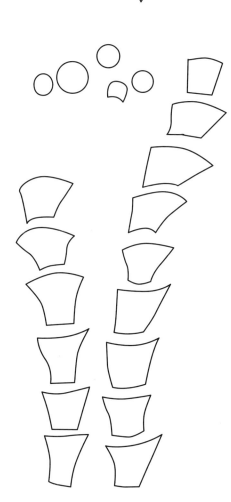

pattern by Annie Lang
pieced by Paris Dukes

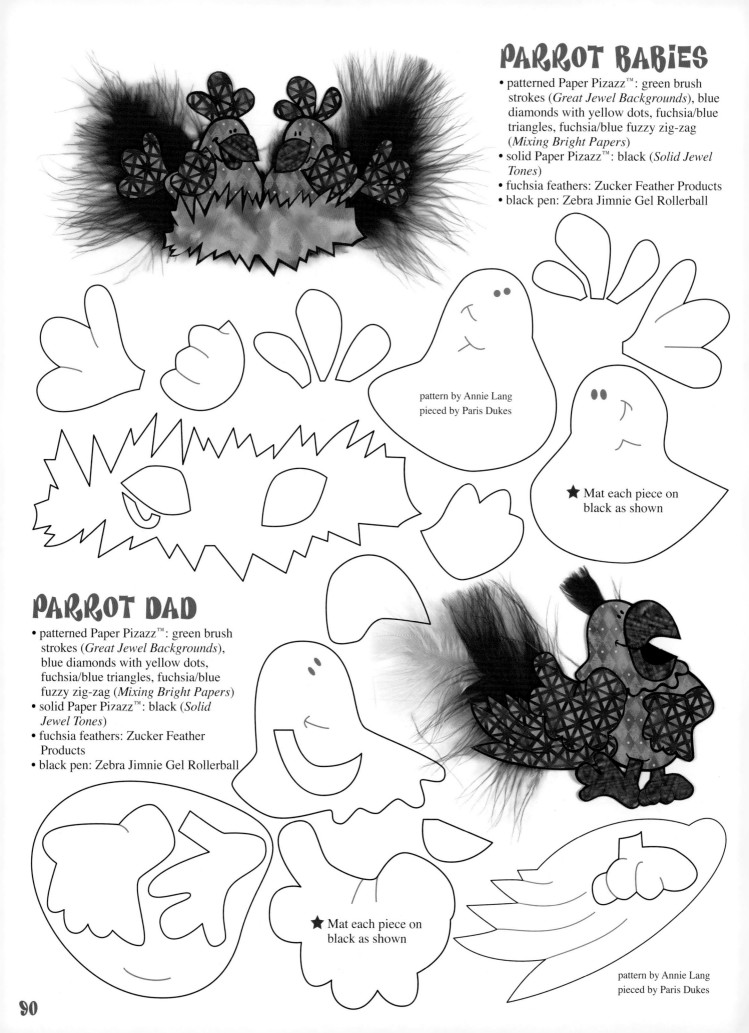

PARROT BABIES

- patterned Paper Pizazz™: green brush strokes (*Great Jewel Backgrounds*), blue diamonds with yellow dots, fuchsia/blue triangles, fuchsia/blue fuzzy zig-zag (*Mixing Bright Papers*)
- solid Paper Pizazz™: black (*Solid Jewel Tones*)
- fuchsia feathers: Zucker Feather Products
- black pen: Zebra Jimnie Gel Rollerball

pattern by Annie Lang
pieced by Paris Dukes

★ Mat each piece on black as shown

PARROT DAD

- patterned Paper Pizazz™: green brush strokes (*Great Jewel Backgrounds*), blue diamonds with yellow dots, fuchsia/blue triangles, fuchsia/blue fuzzy zig-zag (*Mixing Bright Papers*)
- solid Paper Pizazz™: black (*Solid Jewel Tones*)
- fuchsia feathers: Zucker Feather Products
- black pen: Zebra Jimnie Gel Rollerball

★ Mat each piece on black as shown

pattern by Annie Lang
pieced by Paris Dukes

PARROT MOM

- patterned Paper Pizazz™: green brush strokes (*Great Jewel Backgrounds*), blue diamonds with yellow dots, fuchsia/blue triangles, fuchsia/blue fuzzy zig-zag (*Mixing Bright Papers*)
- solid Paper Pizazz™: black (*Solid Jewel Tones*)
- fuchsia feathers: Zucker Feather Products
- black pen: Zebra Jimnie Gel Rollerball

★ Mat each piece on black as shown

pattern by Annie Lang
pieced by Paris Dukes

PENCIL

- patterned Paper Pizazz™: yellow/red gingham, yellow with circles (*Bright Tints*), barnwood*
- specialty Paper Pizazz™: metallic silver* (*Metallic Silver*)
- solid Paper Pizazz™: black (*Solid Jewel Tones*)
- black pen: Zebra Jimnie Gel Rollerball

★ Mat each piece on black as shown
✻ This paper is available by the sheet

pattern by Joy Schaber
pieced by Paris Dukes

PELICANS

- patterned Paper Pizazz™: gray seagull collage, green field collage, brown camera collage (*Masculine Collage Papers*), red sponged (*Mixing Bright Papers*), ivory roses*, barnwood*
- solid Paper Pizazz™: black (*Solid Jewel Tones*)
- black, red, tan decorating chalks: Craf-T Products
- jute twine: Darice
- 1⁄16" wide antique blue satin ribbon: C.M. Offray & Son, Inc.
- black pen: Zebra Jimnie Gel Rollerball
- adhesive foam tape: Therm O Web

★ Mat each piece on black as shown
✳ This paper is available by the sheet

pattern by Annie Lang
pieced by Shauna Berglund-Immel

PiANO

- specialty Paper Pizazz™: black/metallic gold floral, metallic gold* (*Metallic Gold*)
- solid Paper Pizazz™: black (*Solid Jewel Tones*)
- black pen: Zebra Jimnie Gel Rollerball

★ Mat each piece on black as shown
✻ This paper is available by the sheet

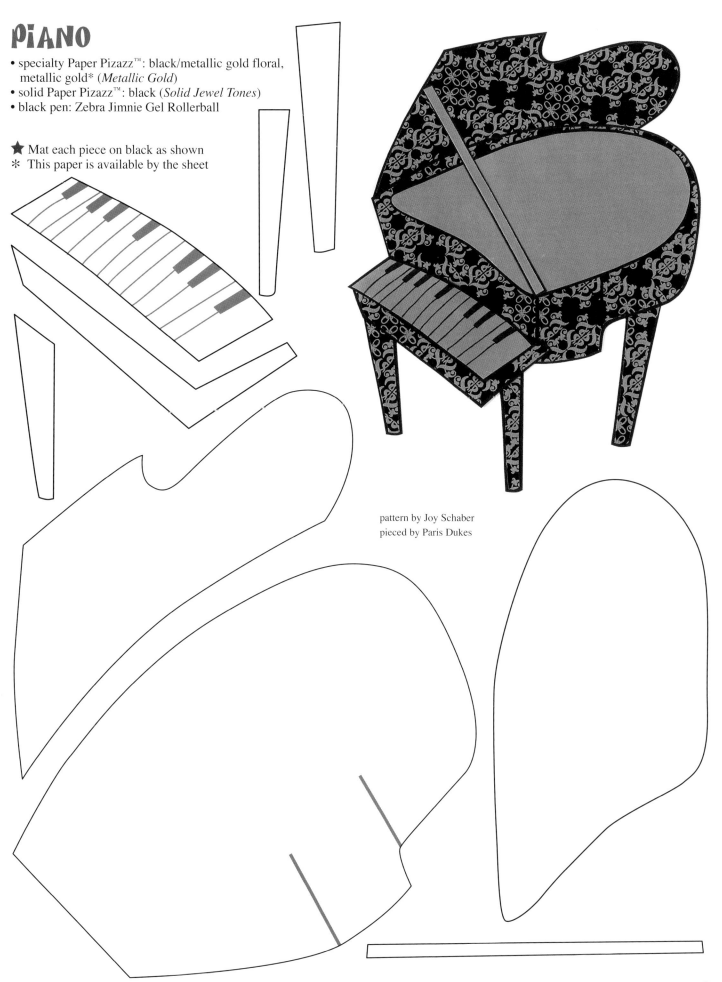

pattern by Joy Schaber
pieced by Paris Dukes

PIE

- patterned Paper Pizazz™: tan mosaic, tan speckled (*Soft & Subtle Textures*)
- specialty Paper Pizazz™: metallic silver (*Metallic Silver*, also by the sheet)
- solid Paper Pizazz™: black (*Solid Jewel Tones*)
- clear micro beads: Magic Scraps™
- brown deocrating chalk: Craf-T Products
- black pen: Zebra Jimnie Gel Rollerball

★ Mat each piece on black as shown

pattern by Joy Schaber
pieced by Paris Dukes

POM POM

- patterned Paper Pizazz™: yellow dots* (*Soft Tints*)
- solid Paper Pizazz™: black (*Solid Jewel Tones*)
- yellow glitter: Magic Scraps™
- black pen: Zig® Writer
- adhesive foam tape: Therm O Web

★ Mat each piece on black as shown
✳ This paper is available by the sheet

pattern by Joy Schaber
pieced by Paris Dukes

PORPOISE

- patterned Paper Pizazz™: purple/blue/white swirls, purple/blue/white brush strokes (*Great Jewel Backgrounds*)
- solid Paper Pizazz™: black (*Solid Jewel Tones*)
- red deocrating chalk: Craf-T Products
- black, white pens: Sakura Gelly Roll

★ Mat each piece on black as shown

pattern by Annie Lang
pieced by Shauna Berglund-Immel

PRINCESS HAT & WAND

- specialty Paper Pizazz™: metallic pink with dots, metallic silver* (*Metallic Silver*)
- solid Paper Pizazz™: black (*Solid Jewel Tones*)
- fibers: Adornaments™
- silver embroidery floss: DMC
- rhinestones: Magic Scraps™

pattern by Joy Schaber
pieced by Paris Dukes

★ Mat each piece on black as shown
＊ This paper is available by the sheet

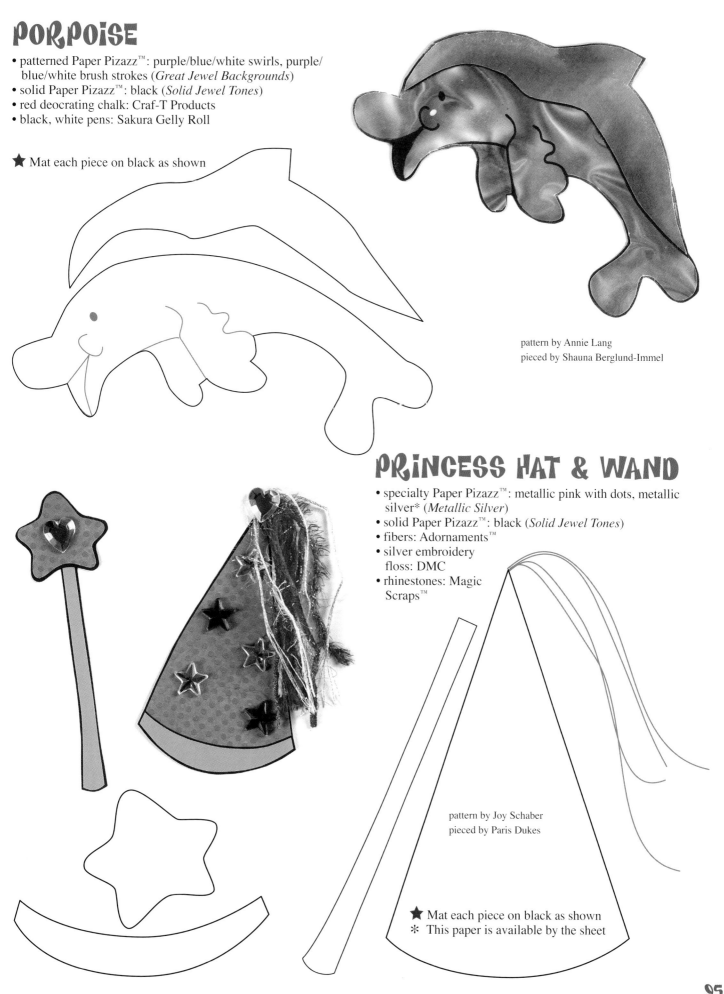

95

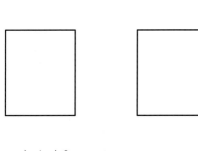

PULL TOY, LAMB

- patterned Paper Pizazz™: black with white dots* (*Heritage Papers*)
- solid Paper Pizazz™: white, pale yellow (*Plain Pastels*), black (*Solid Jewel Tones*)
- orange gingham buttons: Dress It Up
- pink heart bead: Westrim® Crafts
- ³⁄₁₆" wide pink satin picot trim ribbon: C.M. Offray & Son, Inc.
- pink decorating chalk: Craf-T Products
- jute twine: Darice
- black, white pens: Sakura Gelly Roll

★ Mat each piece on black as shown
✳ This paper is available by the sheet

pattern by Annie Lang
pieced by Shauna Berglund-Immel

PULL TOY, TURTLE

- patterned Paper Pizazz™: blue with green dots, blue texture, blue/green stripes (*Mixing Baby Papers*), barnwood*
- solid Paper Pizazz™: black (*Solid Jewel Tones*)
- green heart buttons: Dress It Up
- green fiber: Adornaments™
- white embroidery floss: DMC
- red decorating chalk: Craf-T Products
- black, white pens: Sakura Gelly Roll

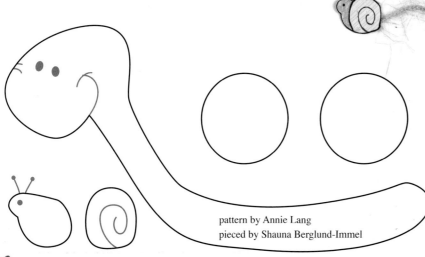

★ Mat each piece on black as shown
✳ This paper is available by the sheet

pattern by Annie Lang
pieced by Shauna Berglund-Immel

PUPPY HIKING

- patterned Paper Pizazz™: red swirl, brown diamonds, green plaid, purple triangles (*Jewel Tints*)
- solid Paper Pizazz™: black (*Solid Jewel Tones*), brown, brown handmade (*Solid Muted Colors*)
- black pen: Zebra Jimnie Gel Rollerball

★ Outline each piece with black as shown

pattern by Annie Lang
pieced by Paris Dukes

PURSE

- specialty Paper Pizazz™: black with metallic silver floral, metallic silver* (*Metallic Silver*)
- 24-gauge wire: Artistic Wire Ltd.
- hematite beads: Blue Moon Beads/ Elizabeth Ward & Co., Inc.

★ Mat each piece on silver as shown
✳ This paper is available by the sheet

pieced by Paris Dukes

pieced by Paris Dukes

QUILT BLOCK #1

- patterned Paper Pizazz™: pale green with pink buttons, pale pink with butterflies, pink gingham (*Mixing Baby Papers*)
- solid Paper Pizazz™: mint green (*Plain Pastels*)
- pink button: Magic Scraps™
- mint green embroidery floss: DMC

★ Mat each piece on mint green as shown

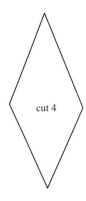

cut 4

QUILT BLOCK #2

- patterned Paper Pizazz™: black with dark pink dots, dark pink with swirls, dark pink with hearts, dark pink with dots/circles, dark pink/pink stripes (*Jewel Tints*)
- solid Paper Pizazz™: black (*Solid Jewel Tones*)
- black button: Magic Scraps™
- black embroidery floss: DMC

★ Mat each piece on black as shown

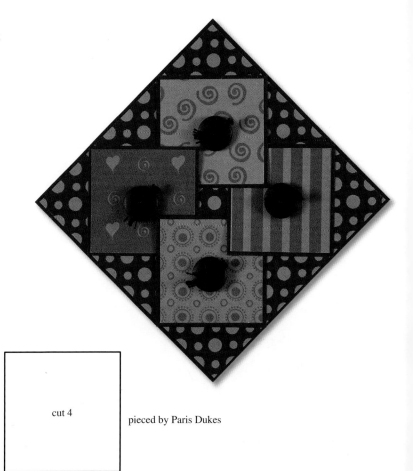

cut 4

pieced by Paris Dukes

QUILTED SNOWFLAKE

- patterned Paper Pizazz™: blue snowflakes, blue plaid with dots, blue with lines/dots (*Mixing Christmas Papers*)
- specialty Paper Pizazz™: metallic silver* (*Metallic Silver*)
- silver snowflake charm: S. Axelrod Company

★ Mat each piece on silver as shown
✽ This paper is available by the sheet

pieced by Paris Dukes

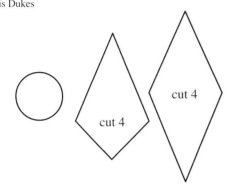

REINDEER WITH LIGHTS

- patterned Paper Pizazz™: red with X's (*Mixing Christmas*), tan webbing, tan sponged (*Soft & Subtle Textures*), crushed suede* (*For Black & White Photos*)
- solid Paper Pizazz™: black (*Solid Jewel Tones*)
- jingle bells: Westrim® Crafts
- lights: Darice
- black pen: Zebra Jimnie Gel Rollerball
- adhesive dots: Glue Dots™

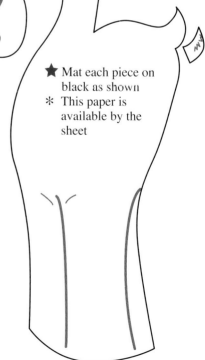

★ Mat each piece on black as shown
✽ This paper is available by the sheet

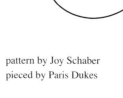

pattern by Joy Schaber
pieced by Paris Dukes

ROOSTER

- patterned Paper Pizazz™: blue paisley, green floral, mauve paisley (*Muted Tints*)
- solid Paper Pizazz™: black, dark mauve, dark tan (*Solid Jewel Tones*)
- black pen: Zebra Jimnie Gel Rollerball
- white pen: Pentel Milky Lunar Gel Roller

★ Mat each piece on black as shown

pattern by Joy Schaber
pieced by Paris Dukes

100

SANTA'S SLEIGH

- patterned Paper Pizazz™: red texture, gold diamonds, tan/red/green plaid, small red holly stripe, tan/red poinsettias, green with fleur de lis (*Mixing Christmas Papers*)
- specialty Paper Pizazz™: metallic gold* (*Metallic Gold*)
- solid Paper Pizazz™: black (*Solid Jewel Tones*)
- ⅛" wide green satin ribbon with gold edges: Ribbon Boutique
- ⅛" wide metallic gold ribbon: C.M. Offray & Son, Inc.
- black pen: Zebra Jimnie Gel Rollerball

★ Mat each piece on black as shown
✳ This paper is available by the sheet

pattern by Joy Schaber
pieced by Paris Dukes

SCHOOL BOOKS

- patterned Paper Pizazz™: yellow dots, yellow gingham, red/yellow wavy plaid, red with yellow dots (*Bright Tints*)
- solid Paper Pizazz™: black (*Solid Jewel Tones*), white (*Plain Pastels*)
- black pen: Zebra Jimmie Gel Rollerball

★ Mat each piece on black as shown

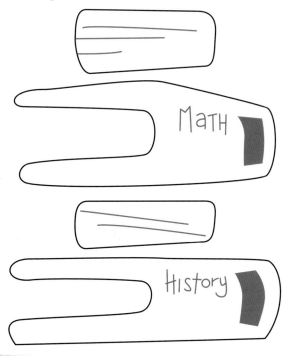

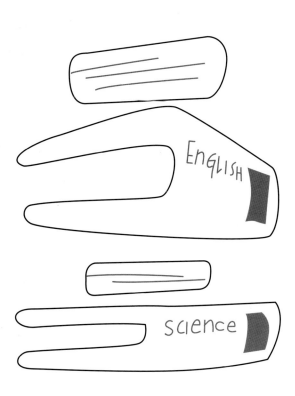

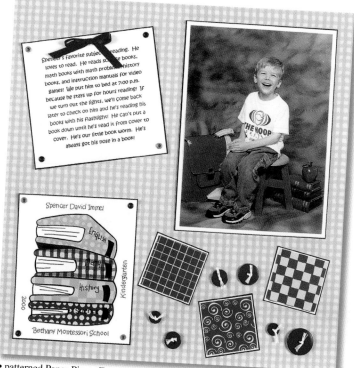

pattern by Joy Schaber
pieced by Paris Dukes
page by Shauna Berglund-Immel

- patterned Paper Pizazz™: yellow gingham, red grid (*Bright Tints,* also by the sheet), red/yellow check, red with yellow swirls (*Bright Tints*)
- solid Paper Pizazz™: white (*Plain Pastels*), black (*Solid Jewel Tones*)
- buttons, eyelets: Magic Scraps™
- white embroidery floss: DMC
- ¼" wide red satin ribbon: C.M. Offray & Son Inc.

SEAPLANE

- patterned Paper Pizazz™: yellow dots, blue dots, green squares, blue swirls* (*Bright Tints*)
- vellum Paper Pizazz™: white* (*Vellum Papers*)
- solid Paper Pizazz™: black (*Solid Jewel Tones*)
- 18-gauge black wire: Artistic Wire Ltd.
- yellow snap: Making Memories™
- black pen: Zebra Jimnie Gell Rollerball

★ Mat each piece on black as shown
★ Outline vellumm with black as shown
✳ This paper is available by the sheet

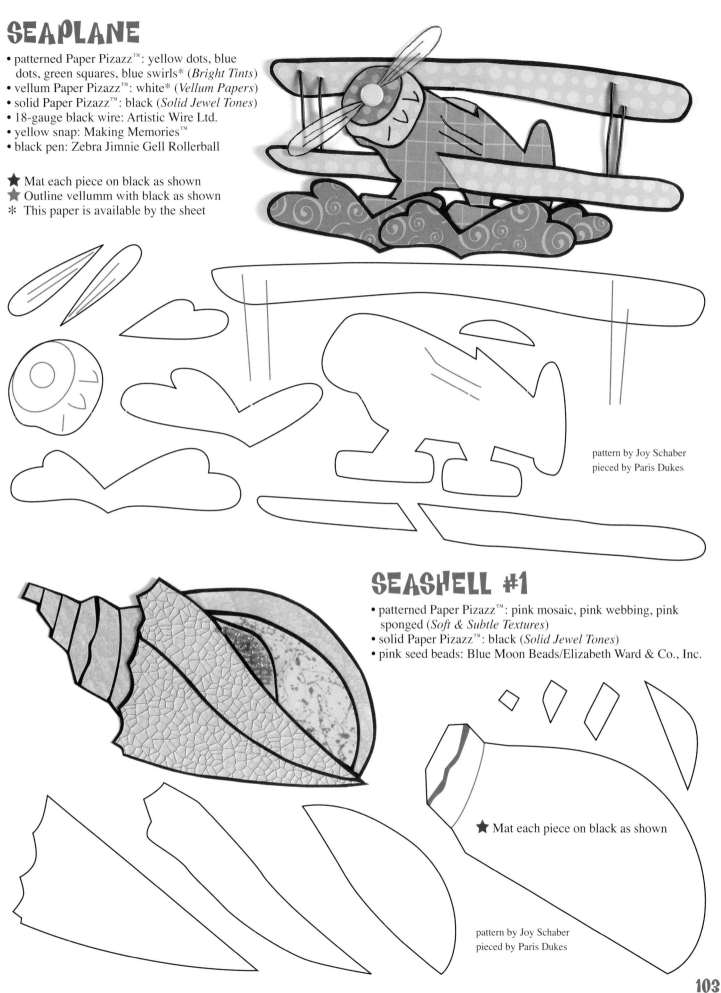

pattern by Joy Schaber
pieced by Paris Dukes

SEASHELL #1

- patterned Paper Pizazz™: pink mosaic, pink webbing, pink sponged (*Soft & Subtle Textures*)
- solid Paper Pizazz™: black (*Solid Jewel Tones*)
- pink seed beads: Blue Moon Beads/Elizabeth Ward & Co., Inc.

★ Mat each piece on black as shown

pattern by Joy Schaber
pieced by Paris Dukes

103

SEASHELL #2

- patterned Paper Pizazz™: lavender mosaic, lavender webbing, lavender sponged (*Soft & Subtle Textures*)
- solid Paper Pizazz™: black (*Solid Jewel Tones*)
- purple seed beads: Blue Moon Beads/Elizabeth Ward & Co., Inc.

⭐ Mat each piece on black as shown

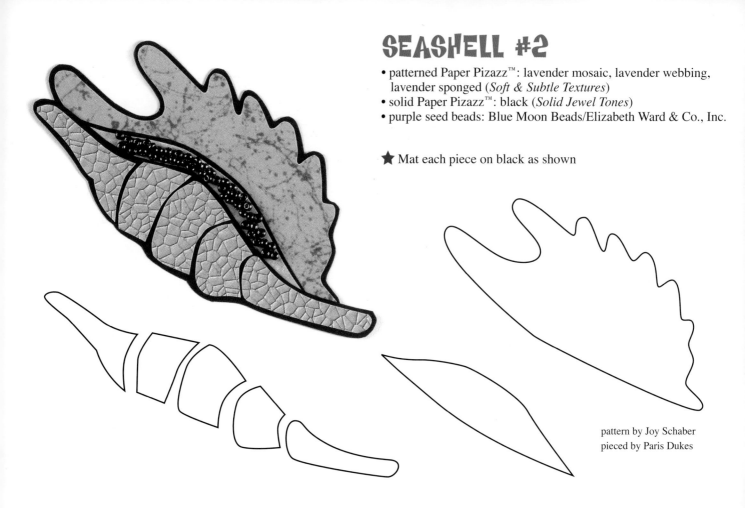

pattern by Joy Schaber
pieced by Paris Dukes

SEASHELL #3

- patterned Paper Pizazz™: tan mosaic, tan webbing, tan sponged (*Soft & Subtle Textures*)
- solid Paper Pizazz™: black (*Solid Jewel Tones*)
- tan seed beads: Blue Moon Beads/Elizabeth Ward & Co., Inc.

⭐ Mat each piece on black as shown

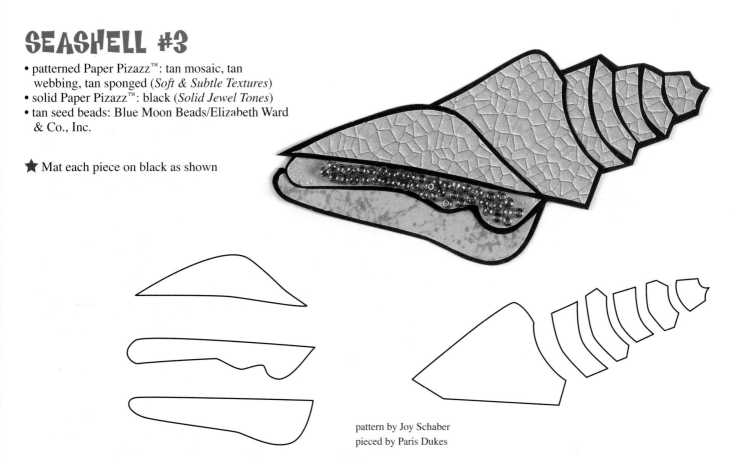

pattern by Joy Schaber
pieced by Paris Dukes

SEASON, FALL

- specialty Paper Pizazz™: metallic gold* (*Metallic Gold*), brown with metallic gold leaves (*Metallic Collage Papers*)
- solid Paper Pizazz™: black (*Solid Jewel Tones*)
- black pen: Zebra Jimnie Gel Rollerball

★ Mat each piece on black as shown
✳ This paper is available by the sheet

pattern by Joy Schaber
pieced by Paris Dukes
page by Arlene Peterson

- specialty Paper Pizazz™: leaf collage (*Metallic Collage Papers*), metallic gold (*Metallic Gold*, also by the sheet)
- solid Paper Pizazz™: black (*Paper Pizazz™ Solid Jewel Tones*)
- gold glitter: Magic Scraps™

Fall is Spencer's favorite Time of the year. He anxiously awaits for the day Daddy rakes the leaves. That means Spencer gets to jump and roll in them!

SEASON, SPRING

- patterned Paper Pizazz™: green/pink floral, green/pink plaid (*Mixing Soft Patterned Papers*)
- solid Paper Pizazz™: black (*Solid Jewel Tones*)
- 24-gauge black wire: Artistic Wire Ltd.
- black eyelets: Stamp Studio

★ Mat each piece on black as shown

To make springs, wrap the wire around a round pencil or paintbrush handle then slip off.

pattern by Joy Schaber
pieced by Paris Dukes

SEASON, SUMMER

- patterned Paper Pizazz™: tan seashells & sand, blue with white seashells (*Vacation Collage*), yellow wavy lines (*Soft Tints*)
- vellum Paper Pizazz™: pastel yellow* (*Pastel Vellum Papers*)
- solid Paper Pizazz™: black (*Solid Jewel Tones*)
- shells: U.S. Shell, Inc.
- black pen: Zebra Jimnie Gel Rollerball

★ Mat each piece except vellum on black as shown
★ Outline vellum with black as shown
✳ This paper is available by the sheet

pattern by Joy Schaber
pieced by Paris Dukes

- patterned Paper Pizazz™: blue with white snowflakes, green/gold plaid with snowflakes (*Mixing Christmas Papers*)
- solid Paper Pizazz™: pale yellow (*Plain Pastels*), black (*Solid Jewel Tones*)
- gold snowflake charms: S. Axelrod Company
- brown decorating chalk: Craf-T Products
- black pen: Zebra Jimnie Gel Rollerball
- orange pen: Pentel Milky Gel Roller

★ Mat each piece on black as shown

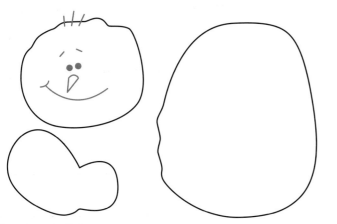

pattern by Joy Schaber
pieced by Paris Dukes

SEED PACKETS

- patterned Paper Pizazz™: white with pink speckles, pink hearts & floral, pink floral (*Lisa Williams, Pink Lavender & Blue*), white with green speckles, green hearts & floral, white with green circles (*Lisa Williams Blue, Yellow & Green*), best buds*
- solid Paper Pizazz™: black (*Solid Jewel Tones*), pastel green (*Plain Pastels*)
- black pen: Zebra Jimnie Gel Rollerball

★ Mat each piece on black as shown

✳ This paper is available by the sheet

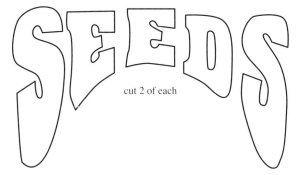

cut 2 of each

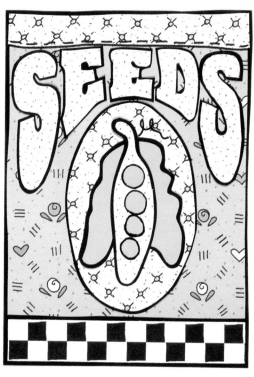

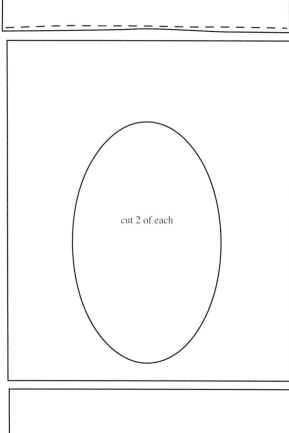

cut 2 of each

pattern by Jacie Pete
pieced by Paris Dukes

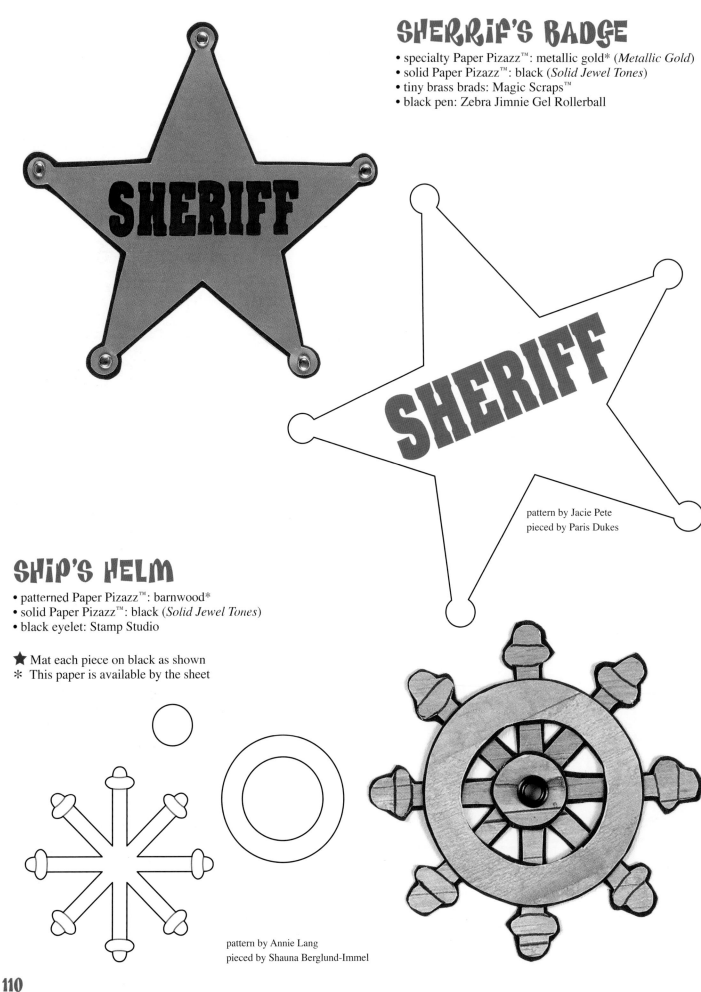

SHERIFF'S BADGE

- specialty Paper Pizazz™: metallic gold* (*Metallic Gold*)
- solid Paper Pizazz™: black (*Solid Jewel Tones*)
- tiny brass brads: Magic Scraps™
- black pen: Zebra Jimnie Gel Rollerball

SHERIFF

pattern by Jacie Pete
pieced by Paris Dukes

SHIP'S HELM

- patterned Paper Pizazz™: barnwood*
- solid Paper Pizazz™: black (*Solid Jewel Tones*)
- black eyelet: Stamp Studio

★ Mat each piece on black as shown
✳ This paper is available by the sheet

pattern by Annie Lang
pieced by Shauna Berglund-Immel

110

SKATEBOARD

- patterned Paper Pizazz™: Girl Power*, blue checks & swirls* (*A Girl's Scrapbook*)
- specialty Paper Pizazz™: metallic silver* (*Metallic Silver*)
- solid Paper Pizazz™: black (*Solid Jewel Tones*)
- silver snaps: Making Memories™
- black pen: Zebra Jimnie Gel Rollerball

★ Mat each piece on black as shown
✳ This paper is available by the sheet

pattern by Joy Schaber
pieced by Paris Dukes

SKI BOAT, WATER SKI & TOW ROPE

- patterned Paper Pizazz™: purpel stars, teal stars, teal water/swirls (*Bright Great Backgrounds*)
- vellum Paper Pizazz™: white swirls* (*Vellum Papers*)
- solid Paper Pizazz™: black (*Solid Jewel Tones*)
- silver brad, black fibers: Magic Scraps™
- 24-gauge silver wire: Artistic Wire Ltd.
- black pen: Zebra Jimnie Gel Rollerball

★ Mat each piece on black as shown
✳ This paper is available by the sheet

pattern by Joy Schaber
pieced by Paris Dukes

SKI CAP

- patterned Paper Pizazz™: dark blue with snowflakes (*Mixing Christmas Papers*), light blue with snowflakes (*Christmas Collage*)
- solid Paper Pizazz™: black (*Solid Jewel Tones*)
- fibers: Magic Scraps™
- pom poms: Westrim® Crafts
- blue decorating chalks: Craf-T Products

★ Mat each piece on black as shown

pieced by Paris Dukes

SNOW CHILD

- patterned Paper Pizazz™: red sponged, yellow grid (*Mixing Bright Papers*)
- solid Paper Pizazz™: black (*Solid Jewel Tones*)
- red buttons, white shaved ice glitter: Magic Scraps™
- pom pom: Westrim® Crafts
- red decorating chalks: Craf-T Products
- white, black pens: Sakura Gelly Roll
- orange pen: Zig® Writer
- adhesive foam tape: Therm O Web

pattern by Annie Lang
pieced by Shauna Berglund-Immel

SNOW GLOBE

- patterned Paper Pizazz™: cream with branches, patchwork with Santa border, cream plaid with stars & snowflakes (*Mixing Christmas Papers*), barnwood*
- vellum Paper Pizazz™: ivory*
- solid Paper Pizazz™: black (*Solid Jewel Tones*)
- clear micro beads: Magic Scraps™
- black pen: Zebra Jimnie Gel Rollerball

⭐ Mat each piece on black as shown
⭐ Outline vellum with black

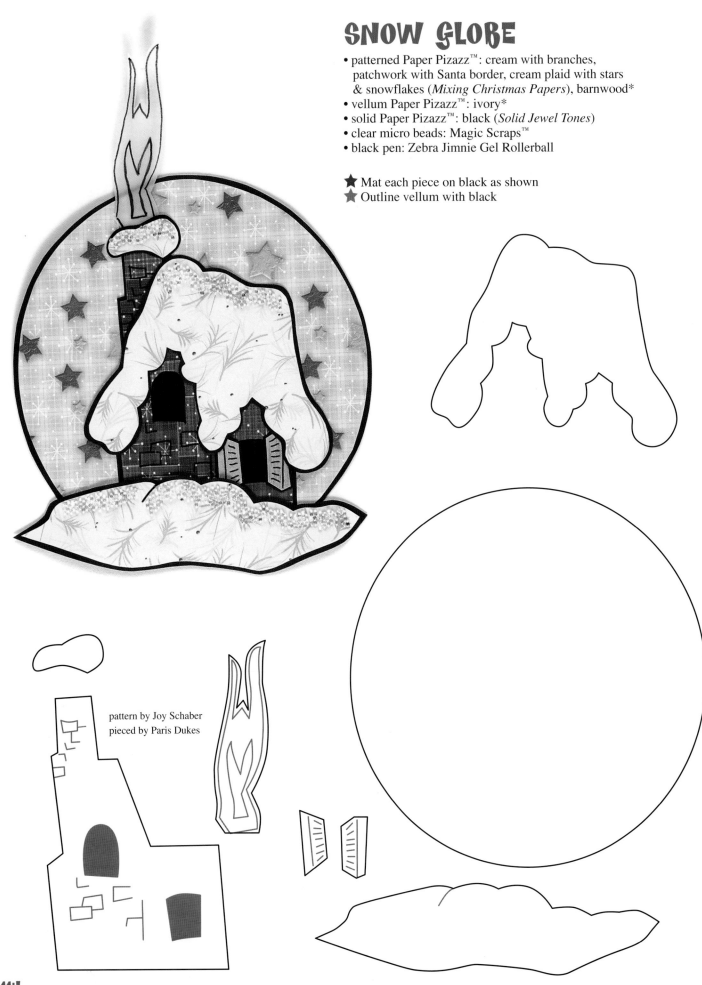

pattern by Joy Schaber
pieced by Paris Dukes

SNOW LADY #1

- patterned Paper Pizazz™: red with X's, patchwork with snowflakes (*Mixing Christmas Papers*), tan mosaic (*Soft & Subtle Textures*)
- solid Paper Pizazz™: black (*Solid Jewel Tones*), pastel yellow (*Plain Pastels*), goldenrod (*Plain Brights*)
- 18-gauge black wire: Artistic Wire Ltd.
- black embroidery floss: DMC
- buttons: Dress It Up
- black seed beads: Blue Moon Beads/Elizabeth Ward & Co., Inc.
- brown, pink, orange decorating chalks: Craf-T Products
- black pen: Zebra Jimnie Gel Rollerball

★ Mat each piece on black as shown

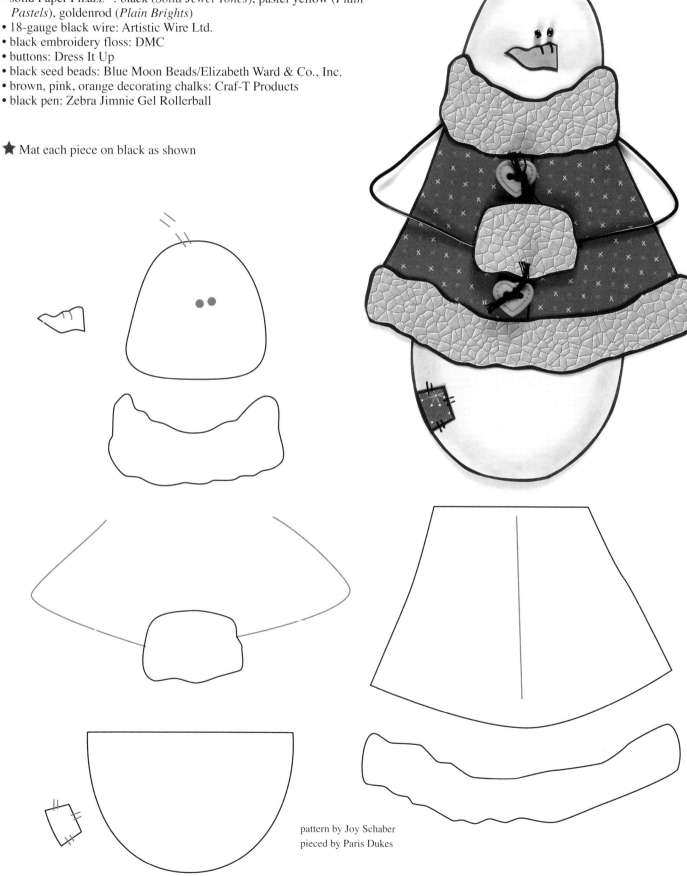

pattern by Joy Schaber
pieced by Paris Dukes

SNOW MAN #1

- patterned Paper Pizazz™: green with X's, red/green plaid, plaid patchwork (*Mixing Christmas Papers*), crushed suede* (*For Black & White Photos*)
- solid Paper Pizazz™: black (*Solid Jewel Tones*), pastel yellow (*Plain Pastels*), goldenrod (*Plain Brights*)
- 18-gauge black wire: Artistic Wire Ltd.
- black embroidery floss: DMC
- buttons: Dress It Up
- ⅛" wide red satin ribbon: C.M. Offray & Son, Inc.
- black seed beads: Blue Moon Beads/Elizabeth Ward & Co., Inc.
- brown, orange, black decorating chalks: Craf-T Products
- black pen: Zebra Jimnie Gel Rollerball
- adhesive foam tape: Therm O Web

★ Mat each piece on black as shown

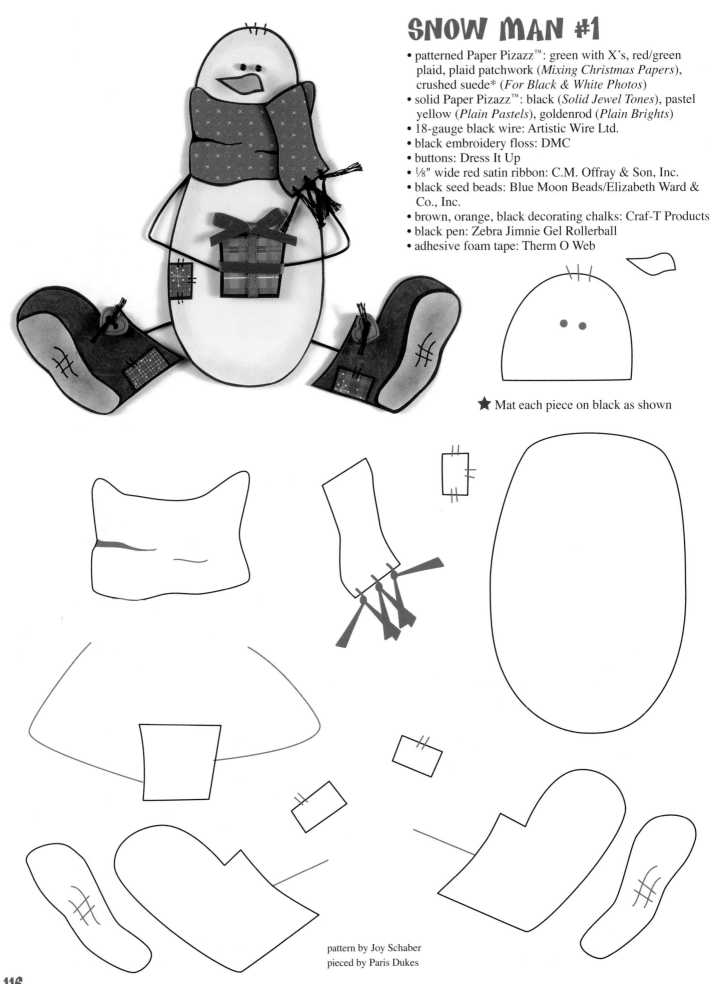

pattern by Joy Schaber
pieced by Paris Dukes

SNOW LADY #2

- patterned Paper Pizazz™: pink brush strokes, lavender knit (*Mixing Baby Papers*),
- solid Paper Pizazz™: black (*Solid Jewel Tones*), white (*Plain Pastels*)
- glitter, buttons: Magic Scraps™
- pure orange pen: Zig® Writer
- black pen: Sakura Gelly Roll
- adhesive foam tape: Therm O Web

★ Mat each piece on black as shown

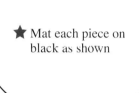
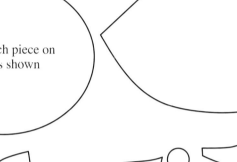

pattern by Annie Lang
pieced by Shauna Berglund-Immel

SNOW MAN #2

- patterned Paper Pizazz™: blue plaid, green with white dots, yellow with sunflowers (*Mixing Soft Patterned Papers*)
- solid Paper Pizazz™: black (*Solid Jewel Tones*), white (*Plain Pastels*)
- red deocrating chalk: Craf-T Products
- black, white pens: Sakura Gelly Roll
- salmon, pure orange pens: Zig® Writer

★ Mat each piece on black as shown

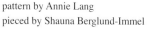

pattern by Annie Lang
pieced by Shauna Berglund-Immel

SOCCER BALL

- patterned Paper Pizazz™: black/teal grid, teal circles, (*Jewel Tints*)
- solid Paper Pizazz™: black (*Solid Jewel Tones*), white (*Plain Pastels*)
- black pen: Zebra Jimnie Gel Rollerball

★ Mat each piece on black as shown

TIGARD SOCCER CLUB

After a rough season last year, Brittany and Monica were determined to work hard and make a difference this year. They worked out together in the off season, conditioning and working on speed, agility and quickness skills. They set personal and team goals. They used visualization techniques their coach taught them. When they weren't netting the books and sleeping, the girls worked on their soccer skills, sacrificing the normal teenager events and adventures. Today that hard work paid off. Today they won the State Championship. Today they saw their goals realized. Their visualizations play out. Today they celebrated their journey together. Today is only the beginning of a lifetime full of success. Tonight they will set new goals.

Fall Season 2002

- patterned Paper Pizazz™: teal dots, black grid, teal gingham (*Jewel Tints*)
- solid Paper Pizazz™: white (*Plain Pastels*), black (*Paper Pizazz*™ *Solid Jewel Tones*)
- netting, tinsel: Magic Scraps™

pattern by Joy Schaber
pieced by Paris Dukes
page by Shauna Berglund-Immel

118

THE SPACE NEEDLE

- patterned Paper Pizazz™: blue sponged, purple grid, blue/purple stripe (*Mixing Masculine*)
- vellum Paper Pizazz™: pastel blue* (*Pastel Vellum Papers*)
- solid Paper Pizazz™: black (*Solid Jewel Tones*)
- black pen: Zebra Jimnie Gel Rollerball

★ Mat each piece on black as shown, except vellum

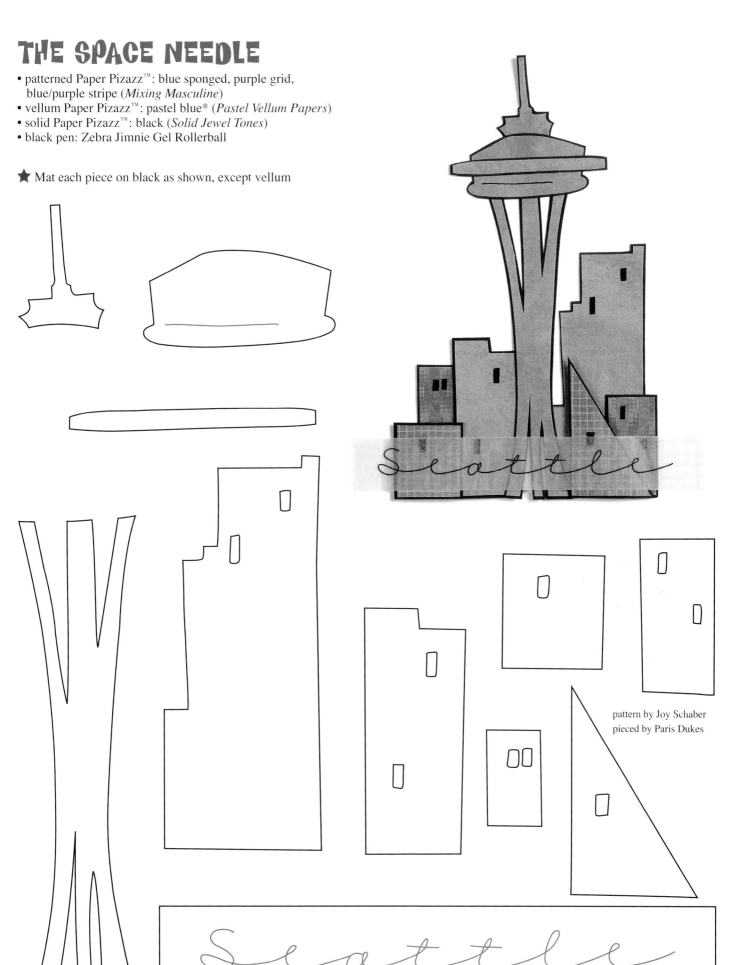

pattern by Joy Schaber
pieced by Paris Dukes

SQUIRREL WITH ACORN

- patterned Paper Pizazz™: brown squares, brown circles, brown diamonds, green checks (*Jewel Tints*)
- solid Paper Pizazz™: black (*Solid Jewel Tones*)
- white pen: Pentel Milky Lunar Gel
- black pen: Zebra Jimnie Gel Rollerball

★ Mat each piece on black as shown

pattern by Joy Schaber
pieced by Paris Dukes

STATUE OF LIBERTY

- patterned Paper Pizazz™: butterflies*, white satin*
- solid Paper Pizazz™: black (*Solid Jewel Tones*)
- glitter: Magic Scraps™
- black pen: Zebra Jimnie Gel Rollerball

★ Mat each piece on black as shown

pattern by Joy Schaber
pieced by Paris Dukes
page by Arlene Peterson

• patterned Paper Pizazz™: purple city collage (*Vacation Collage*)
• specialty Paper Pizazz™: silver (*Metallic Silver*, also by the sheet)
• solid Paper Pizazz™: black (*Solid Jewel Tones*)

STORK WITH BABY

- patterned Paper Pizazz™: blue plaid, yellow plaid, blue blanket texture, blue/yellow stars, pink gingham, "It's a Boy" (*Mixing Baby Papers*)
- solid Paper Pizazz™: black (*Solid Jewel Tones*), white (*Plain Pastels*)
- red decorating chalk: Craf-T Products
- buttons: Magic Scraps™
- red pen: Zig® Writer
- white, black pens: Sakura Gelly Roll

★ Mat each piece on black as shown

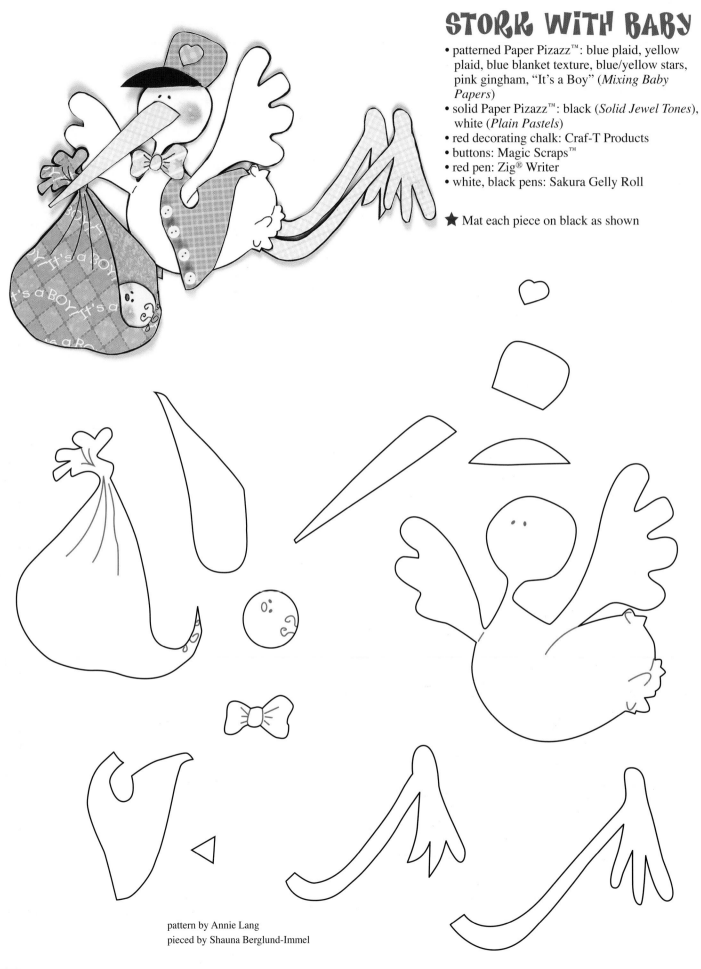

pattern by Annie Lang
pieced by Shauna Berglund-Immel

SUITCASE

- patterned Paper Pizazz™: island paradise with tag (*Masculine Collage Papers*)
- specialty Paper Pizazz™: metallic gold* (*Metallic Gold*)
- solid Paper Pizazz™: black (*Solid Jewel Tones*)
- travel labels: *Stack 'em Cut-Outs*
- key charm: S. Axelrod Co.
- gold eyelet: HyGlo/American Pin
- jute twine: Darice
- brown decorating chalks: Craf-T Products
- gold pen: Hybrid Gel Roller

⭐ Mat each piece on black as shown

pieced by Paris Dukes
page by Arlene Peterson

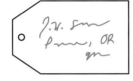

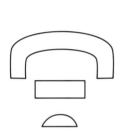

- patterned Paper Pizazz™: island paradise collage (*Masculine Collage*)
- specialty Paper Pizazz™: pastel tan vellum (*Pastel Vellum Papers*, also by the sheet)
- cut-outs: alphabet tags (*Paper Pizazz™ Tag Art #2*)
- solid Paper Pizazz™: black (*Solid Jewel Tones*)
- ⅛" gold brads: Magic Scraps™

SURFER

- patterned Paper Pizazz™: blue/green stripe, blue water (*Bright Great Backgrounds*)
- solid Paper Pizazz™: black (*Solid Jewel Tones*)
- black pen: Zebra Jimnie Gel Rollerball

★ Mat each piece on black as shown

pattern by Joy Schaber
pieced by Paris Dukes

SWIM TRUNKS

- patterned Paper Pizazz™: blue/green diamonds with burgundy dots, burgundy sponged (*Mixing Bright Papers*)
- solid Paper Pizazz™: black (*Solid Jewel Tones*)
- button: Magic Scraps™
- black pen: Zebra Jimnie Gel Rollerball

★ Mat each piece on black as shown

pattern by Joy Schaber
pieced by Paris Dukes

TAJ MAHAL

- patterned Paper Pizazz™: ivory roses*
- specialty Paper Pizazz™: metallic gold*
  (*Metallic Gold*), ivory vellum*
- solid Paper Pizazz™: black (*Solid Jewel Tones*)
- gold eyelets: Stamp Studio
- black pen: Zebra Jimnie Gel Rollerball

★ Mat each piece on black as shown, except vellum

✳ This paper is available by the sheet

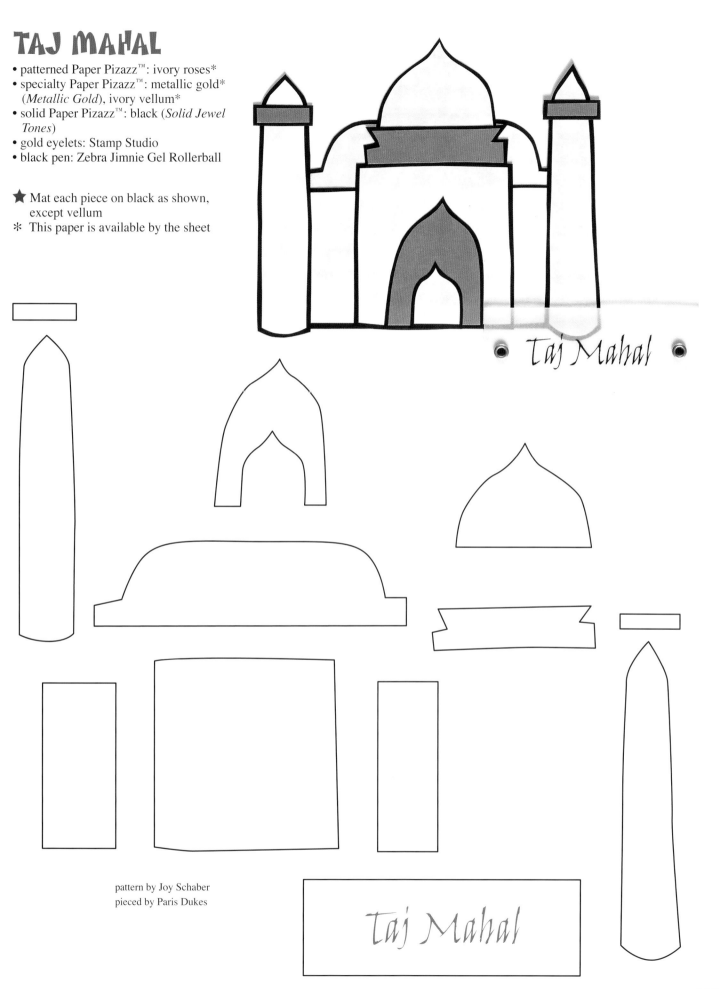

pattern by Joy Schaber
pieced by Paris Dukes

Taj Mahal

TAPE MEASURE

- specialty Paper Pizazz™: metallic silver* (*Metallic Silver*), light blue sponged (*Soft & Subtle Textures*), yellow lined paper*
- solid Paper Pizazz™: black (*Solid Jewel Tones*), yellow (*Plain Pastels*)
- silver snap: Making Memories™
- black pen: Zebra Jimnie Gel Rollerball

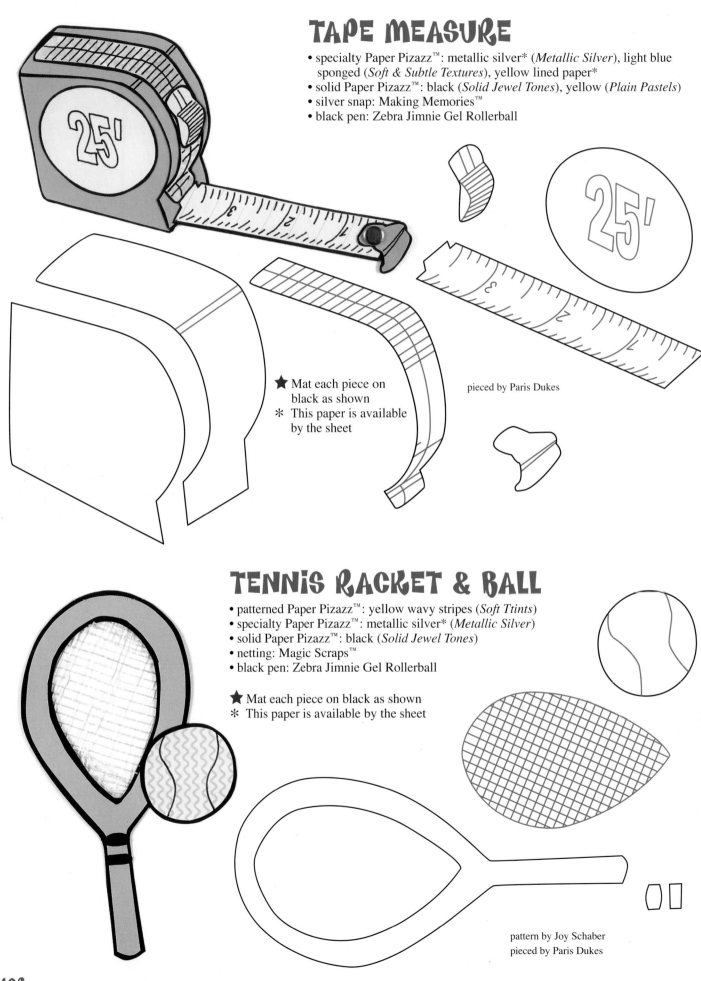

25'

★ Mat each piece on black as shown
✷ This paper is available by the sheet

pieced by Paris Dukes

TENNIS RACKET & BALL

- patterned Paper Pizazz™: yellow wavy stripes (*Soft Ttints*)
- specialty Paper Pizazz™: metallic silver* (*Metallic Silver*)
- solid Paper Pizazz™: black (*Solid Jewel Tones*)
- netting: Magic Scraps™
- black pen: Zebra Jimnie Gel Rollerball

★ Mat each piece on black as shown
✷ This paper is available by the sheet

pattern by Joy Schaber
pieced by Paris Dukes

126

TEPEE

- patterned Paper Pizazz™: brown desert collage, blue desert collage (*Vacation Collage*), barnwood*
- solid Paper Pizazz™: black (*Solid Jewel Tones*)
- black pen: Zebra Jimnie Gel Rollerball

★ Mat each piece on black as shown

✳ This paper is available by the sheet

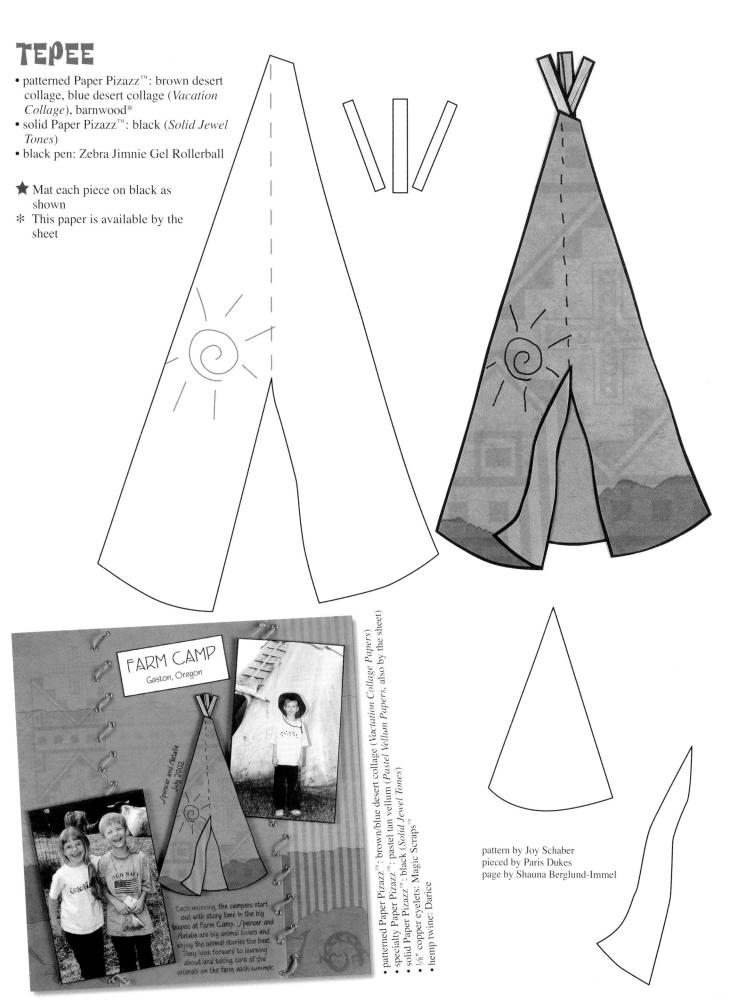

FARM CAMP
Gaston, Oregon

Spencer and Natalie
July 2002

Each morning, the campers start out with story time in the big teepee at Farm Camp. Spencer and Natalie are big animal lovers and enjoy the animal stories the best. They look forward to learning about and taking care of the animals on the farm each summer.

- patterned Paper Pizazz™: brown/blue desert collage (*Vacation Collage Papers*)
- specialty Paper Pizazz™: pastel tan vellum (*Pastel Vellum Papers*, also by the sheet)
- solid Paper Pizazz™: black (*Solid Jewel Tones*)
- ⅛" copper eyelets: Magic Scraps™
- hemp twine: Darice

pattern by Joy Schaber
pieced by Paris Dukes
page by Shauna Berglund-Immel

127

TiGER

- patterned Paper Pizazz™: yellow roses*, brown swirls*
- solid Paper Pizazz™: black (*Solid Jewel Tones*), white (*Plain Pastels*)
- black pen: Sakura Micron

★ Mat each piece on black as shown
✳ This paper is available by the sheet

pattern by Annie Lang
pieced by Toddi Barclay
page by LeNae Gerig

- patterned Paper Pizazz™: navy blue with stars (*12"x12" Dots, Plaids, Checks & Stripes*, also by the sheet), baseballs (*Sports*, also by the sheet)
- solid Paper Pizazz™: white, ivory (*Plain Pastels*), red (*Solid Jewel Tones*)
- 2" circle punch: Marvy® Uchida
- red pen: Zig® Writer

TOOL BOX

- patterned Paper Pizazz™: metallic copper, metallic silver*, metallic gold* (*Heavy Metals*), barnwood*, denim*
- solid Paper Pizazz™: black (*Solid Jewel Tones*)
- gold brads: HyGlo/American Pin
- black pen: Zebra Jimnie Gel Rollerball

★ Mat each piece on black as shown
✳ This paper is available by the sheet

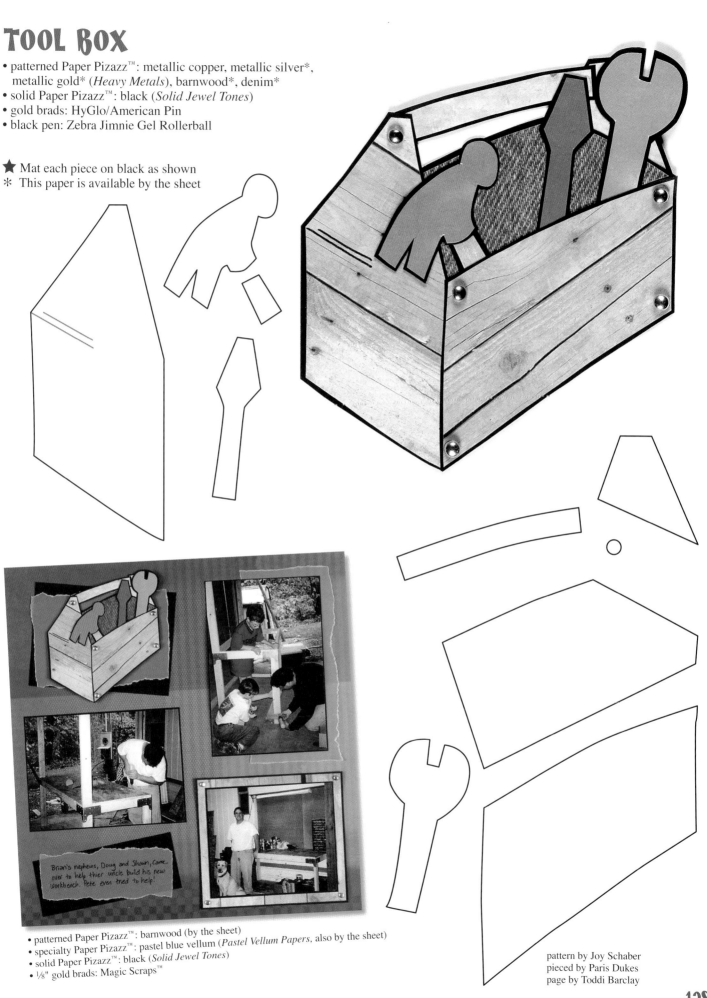

- patterned Paper Pizazz™: barnwood (by the sheet)
- specialty Paper Pizazz™: pastel blue vellum (*Pastel Vellum Papers*, also by the sheet)
- solid Paper Pizazz™: black (*Solid Jewel Tones*)
- ⅛" gold brads: Magic Scraps™

Brian's nephews, Doug and Shawn, came over to help thier uncle build his new Workbench. Pete even tried to help!

pattern by Joy Schaber
pieced by Paris Dukes
page by Toddi Barclay

129

TOTEM POLE

- patterned Paper Pizazz™: brown diamonds, black/brown swirls, red with circles, red swirls, green swirly stripe, green zig-zag (*Jewel Tints*)
- solid Paper Pizazz™: black (*Solid Jewel Tones*), white (*Plain Pastels*)
- feathers: Zucker Feather Products
- black pen: Zebra Jimmie Gel Rollerball

pattern by Joy Schaber
pieced by Paris Dukes

★ Mat each piece on black as shown

130

TRAIN

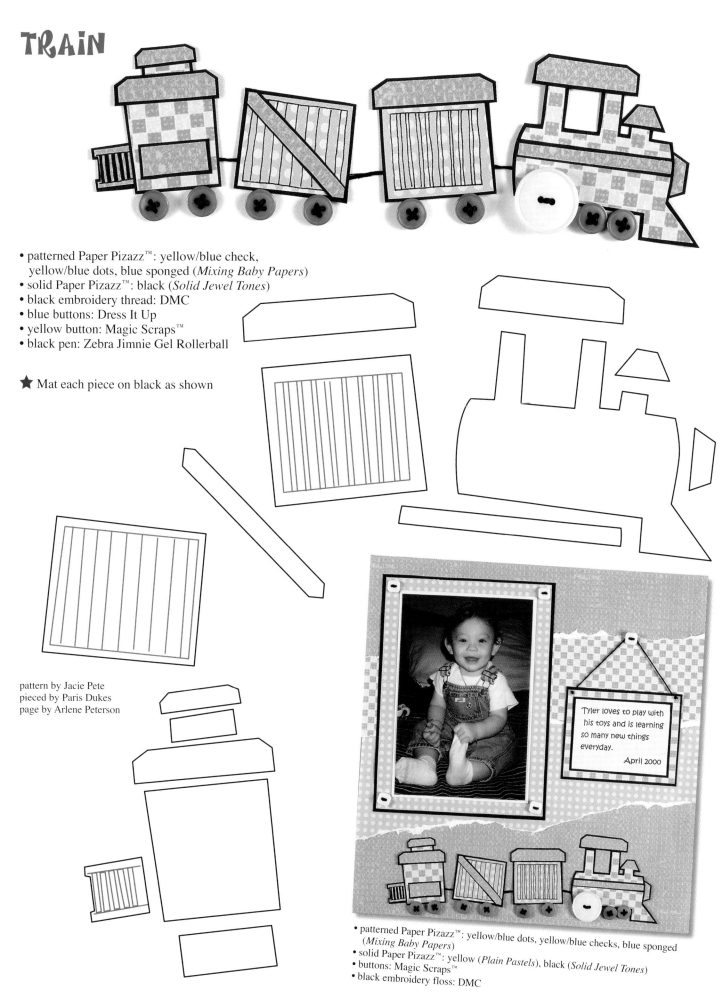

- patterned Paper Pizazz™: yellow/blue check, yellow/blue dots, blue sponged (*Mixing Baby Papers*)
- solid Paper Pizazz™: black (*Solid Jewel Tones*)
- black embroidery thread: DMC
- blue buttons: Dress It Up
- yellow button: Magic Scraps™
- black pen: Zebra Jimnie Gel Rollerball

★ Mat each piece on black as shown

pattern by Jacie Pete
pieced by Paris Dukes
page by Arlene Peterson

Tyler loves to play with his toys and is learning so many new things everyday.

April 2000

- patterned Paper Pizazz™: yellow/blue dots, yellow/blue checks, blue sponged (*Mixing Baby Papers*)
- solid Paper Pizazz™: yellow (*Plain Pastels*), black (*Solid Jewel Tones*)
- buttons: Magic Scraps™
- black embroidery floss: DMC

TREASURE CHEST

- patterned Paper Pizazz™: brown travel collage (*Masculine Collage Papers*)
- specialty Paper Pizazz™: metallic gold* (*Metallic Gold*)
- solid Paper Pizazz™: black (*Solid Jewel Tones*)
- gold brad, gold shaved ice glitter, rhinestones: Magic Scraps™

★ Mat each piece on black as shown
✶ This paper is available by the sheet

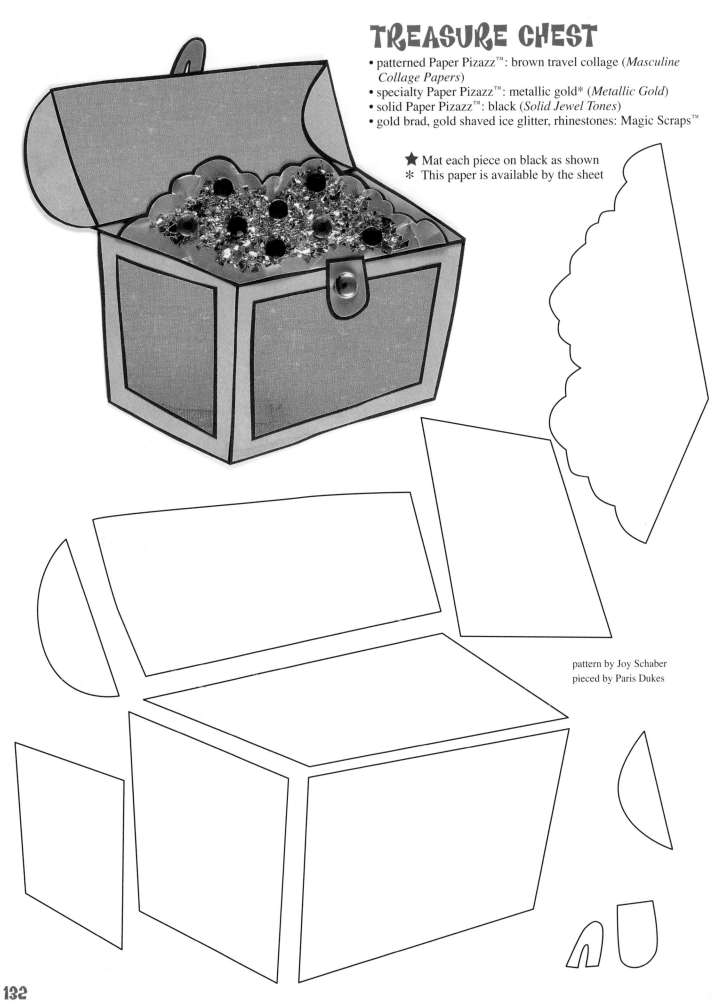

pattern by Joy Schaber
pieced by Paris Dukes

TRUCK

- patterned Paper Pizazz™: blue/green diamonds with dots, burgundy sponged (*Mixing Bright Papers*)
- vellum Paper Pizazz™: white* (*Vellum Papers*)
- solid Paper Pizazz™: black (*Solid Jewel Tones*), white (*Plain Pastels*)
- black embroidery floss: DMC
- black, burgundy buttons: Making Memories™ Details™
- black pen: Sakura Gelly Roll

★ Mat each piece on black as shown
✳ This paper is available by the sheet

pattern by Annie Lang
pieced by Paris Dukes

TRUCK, MONSTER

- patterned Paper Pizazz™: large red swirl, small red swirl (*Great Jewel Backgrounds*)
- specialty Paper Pizazz™: white vellum* (*Vellum Papers*), metallic silver* (*Metallic Silver*)
- solid Paper Pizazz™: black (*Solid Jewel Tones*)
- silver snaps: Making Memories™ Details™
- black pen: Zebra Jimnie Gel Rollerball

★ Mat each piece on black as shown, except vellum and tires
✳ This paper is available by the sheet

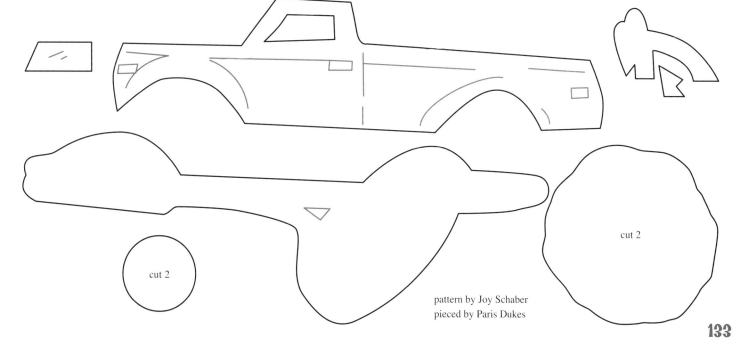

cut 2

cut 2

pattern by Joy Schaber
pieced by Paris Dukes

133

TULIP

- patterned Paper Pizazz™: lavender floral, purple floral, green floral (*12"x12" Muted Tints*)
- solid Paper Pizazz™: black (*Solid Jewel Tones*)
- purple seed beads: Blue Moon Beads/Elizabeth Ward & Co., Inc.
- black pen: Zig® Writer

★ Mat each piece on black as shown

pattern by Joy Schaber
pieced by Paris Dukes
page by Shauna Berglund-Immel

- patterned Paper Pizazz™: purple floral, green floral (*12"x12" Muted Tints*)
- specialty Paper Pizazz™: silver (*Metallic Silver,* also by the sheet), white vellum (*Vellum Papers,* also by the sheet)
- ¼" silver brads: Magic Scraps™
- ⅝" wide sheer lavender ribbon: C.M. Offray & Son Inc.

TULIPS #2

- patterned Paper Pizazz™: purple floral, purple paisley, green floral (*Muted Tints*)
- black pen: Zebra Jimnie Gel Rollerball

★ Outline each piece with black as shown

Woodburn Tulip Festival
April 2001

I love to sit and watch Elise explore the sea of tulips. Her favorites are the purple ones. She looks like a little tulip herself out there amongst the purple buds. I think she's the prettiest flower out there, turning her face towards the sun and blossoming into a beautiful little girl full of wonder and delight.

ELISE

- patterned Paper Pizazz™: purple floral, purple paisley, green stripes (*Muted Tints*)
- specialty Paper Pizazz™: gold (*Metallic Gold*, also by the sheet), white vellum (*Vellum Papers*, also by the sheet), pastel purple vellum (*Pastel Vellum Papers*, also by the sheet)
- cut-outs: alphabet tiles (*Artsy Collage™ Alphabet Tiles*)
- solid Paper Pizazz™: white (*Plain Pastels*)
- ⅝" wide sheer lavender ribbon: C.M. Offray & Son Inc.
- gold pen: Sakura Gelly Roll

pattern by Joy Schaber
pieced by Paris Dukes
page by Shauna Berglund-Immel

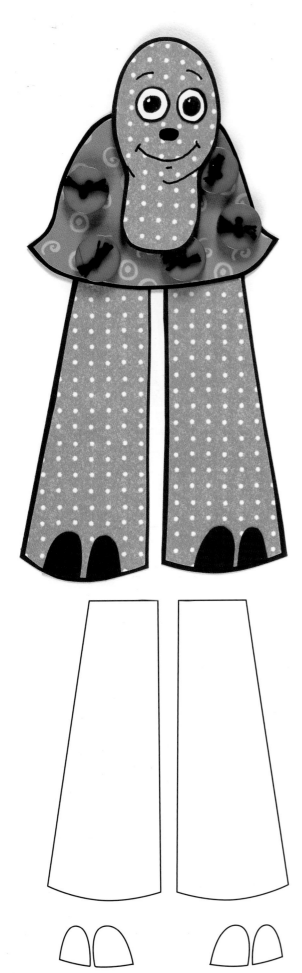

TURTLE

- patterned Paper Pizazz™: green with white dots (*Mixing Soft Patterns*), green swirls (*12"x12" Muted Tints*)
- solid Paper Pizazz™: black (*Solid Jewel Tones*), white (*Plain Pastels*)
- black embroidery floss: DMC
- green buttons: Dress It Up
- black pen: Zebra Jimmie Gel Rollerball
- adhesive foam tape: Therm O Web

★ Mat each paper piece on black as shown

pattern by Joy Schaber
pieced by Paris Dukes
page by LeNae Gerig

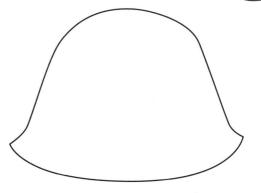

- patterned Paper Pizazz™: blue/green plaid, green swirl, green with white dots (*Mixing Soft Patterned Papers*), bubbles (*Baby's First Year*, also by the sheet)
- specialty Paper Pizazz™: white vellum (*Vellum Papers*, also by the sheet)
- solid Paper Pizazz™: white, light green (*Plain Pastels*)
- ¼" buttons: Magic Scraps™
- black thread

U.S. CAPITOL

- vellum Paper Pizazz™: ivory*
- solid Paper Pizazz™: black (*Solid Jewel Tones*), ivory (*Plain Pastel Papers*)
- black eyelets: Stamp Studio
- brown decorating chalk: Craf-T Products
- black pen: Zebra Jimnie Gel Rollerball

★ Mat each piece on black as shown, except vellum
✳ This paper is available by the sheet

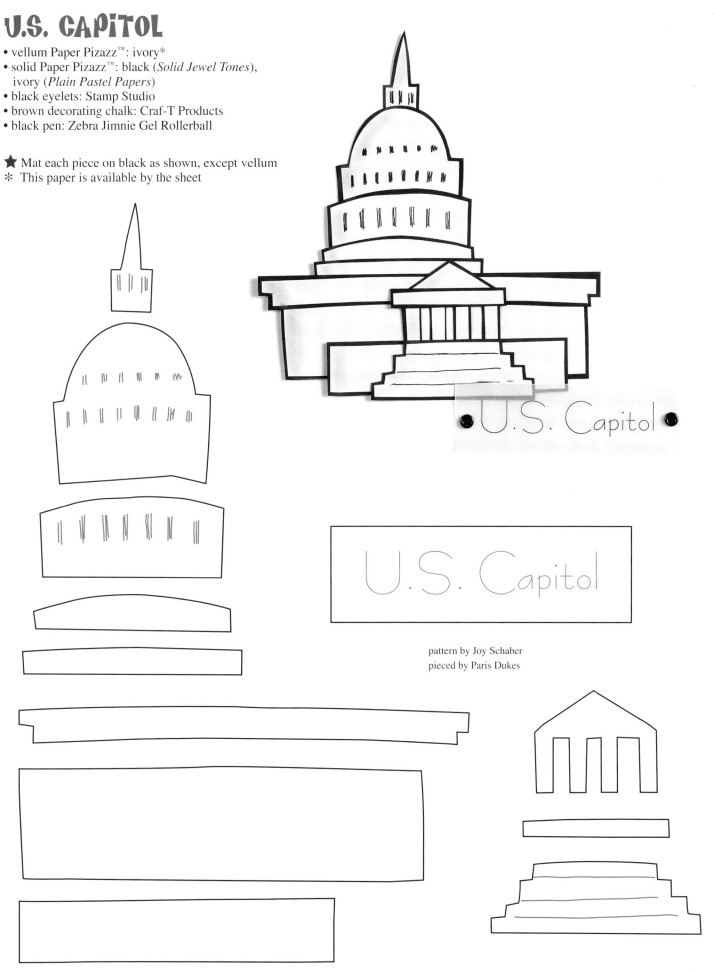

U.S. Capitol

pattern by Joy Schaber
pieced by Paris Dukes

137

VOLCANO

- patterned Paper Pizazz™: red circles, brown diamonds, red swirls (*Jewel Tints*)
- solid Paper Pizazz™: black (*Solid Jewel Tones*)
- red glitter: Magic Scraps™
- black pen: Zebra Jimnie Gel Rollerball

★ Mat each piece on black as shown

pattern by Joy Schaber
pieced by Paris Dukes

WASHINGTON MONUMENT

- patterned Paper Pizazz™: tan/white mosaic with lace border (*Soft Collage Papers*)
- vellum Paper Pizazz™: pastel blue*, pastel yellow* (*Pastel Vellum Papers*), ivory*
- solid Paper Pizazz™: black (*Solid Jewel Tones*)
- black eyelets: Stamp Studio
- black pen: Zebra Jimnie Gel Rollerball

⭐ Mat each paper piece on black as shown
⭐ Outline each vellum piece with black as shown
✳ This paper is available by the sheet

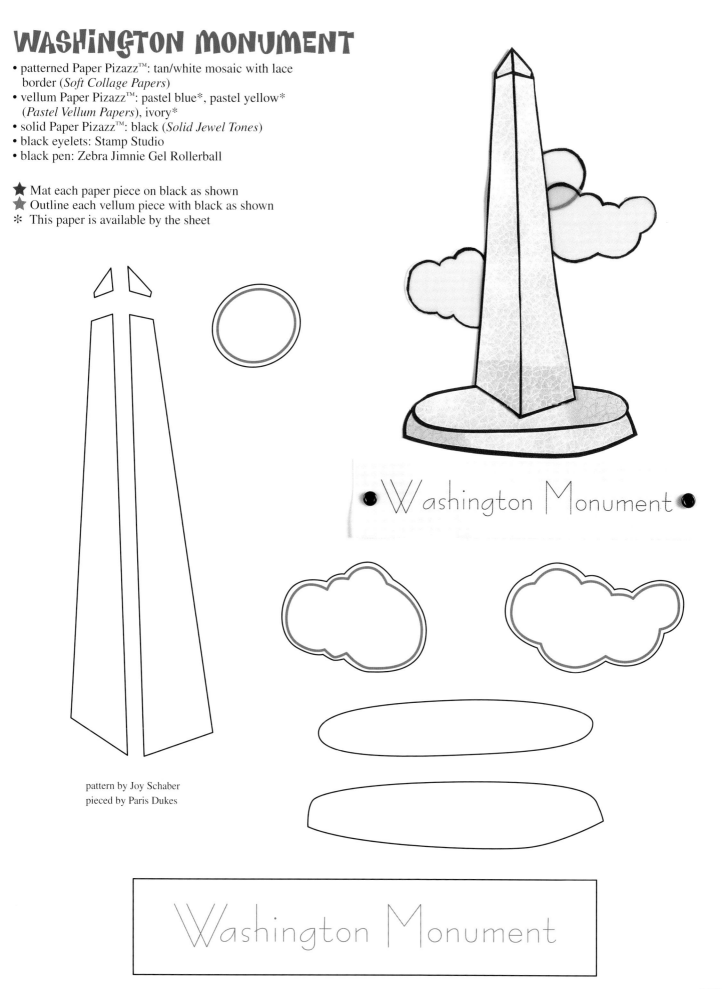

pattern by Joy Schaber
pieced by Paris Dukes

Washington Monument

WATCH

- patterned Paper Pizazz™: tan embossed, tan solid (*"Leather" Papers*)
- specialty Paper Pizazz™: metallic gold* (*Metallic Gold*)
- solid Paper Pizazz™: black (*Solid Jewel Tones*)
- clock charm: S. Axelrod Co.

★ Mat each piece on black as shown
✳ This paper is available by the sheet

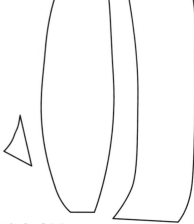

pattern by Joy Schaber
pieced by Paris Dukes

WHALE

- patterned Paper Pizazz™: elephant (*Wild Things*)
- vellum Paper Pizazz™: pastel blue* (*Pastel Vellum Papers*)
- solid Paper Pizazz™: black (*Solid Jewel Tones*)
- black eyelets: Stamp Studio
- red decorating chalk: Craf-T Products
- white, black pens: Sakura Gelly Roll

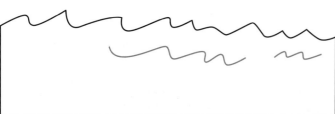

★ Mat each paper piece on black as shown
★ Outline each vellum piece with black as shown
✳ This paper is available by the sheet

pattern by Annie Lang
pieced by Shauna Berglund-Immel

WHEELBARROW

- patterned Paper Pizzazz™: pink floral, blue floral, aqua floral, aqua with leaves (*Muted Tints*), barnwood*
- specialty Paper Pizzazz™: metallic silver* (*Metallic Silver*)
- solid Paper Pizzazz™: black (*Solid Jewel Tones*)
- silver snap, silver flower snaps: Making Memories™

★ Mat each piece on black as shown
✳ This paper is available by the sheet

pattern by Joy Schaber
pieced by Paris Dukes

THE WHITE HOUSE

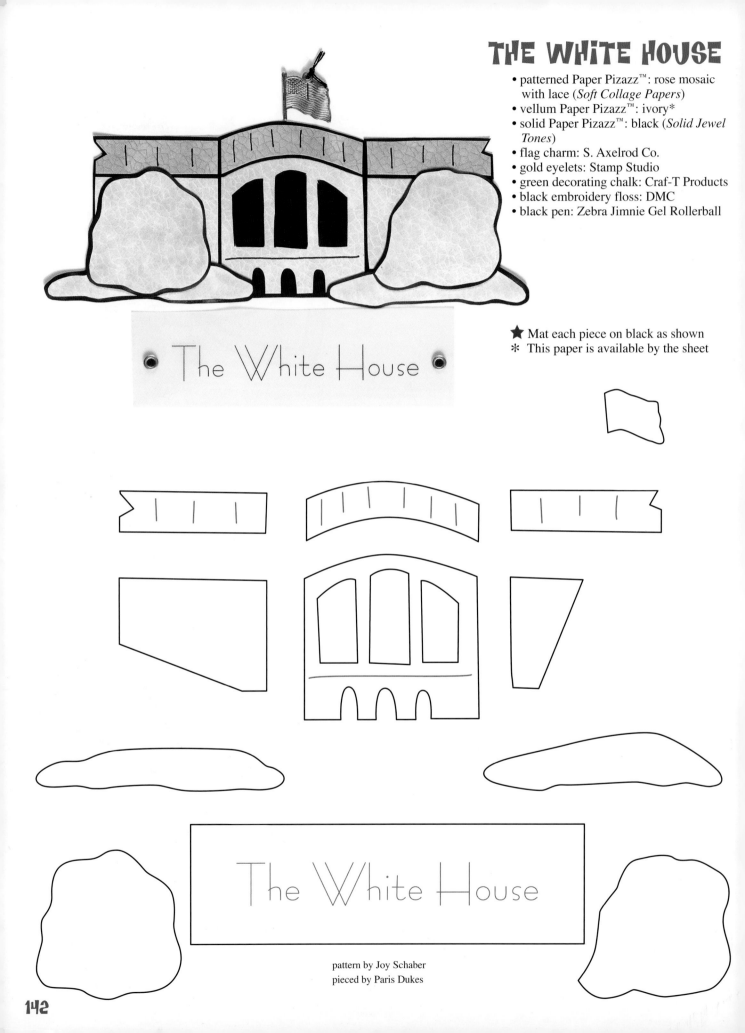

- patterned Paper Pizazz™: rose mosaic with lace (*Soft Collage Papers*)
- vellum Paper Pizazz™: ivory*
- solid Paper Pizazz™: black (*Solid Jewel Tones*)
- flag charm: S. Axelrod Co.
- gold eyelets: Stamp Studio
- green decorating chalk: Craf-T Products
- black embroidery floss: DMC
- black pen: Zebra Jimnie Gel Rollerball

★ Mat each piece on black as shown

✳ This paper is available by the sheet

The White House

The White House

pattern by Joy Schaber
pieced by Paris Dukes

WINDMILL

- patterned Paper Pizazz™: blue/green stripes, blue floral, blue/green tiny stripes, green floral (*Joy's Vintage Papers*)
- solid Paper Pizazz™: black (*Solid Jewel Tones*)
- green snap: Making Memories™
- white pen: Pentel Milky Lunar Gel Roller

★ Mat each piece on black as shown

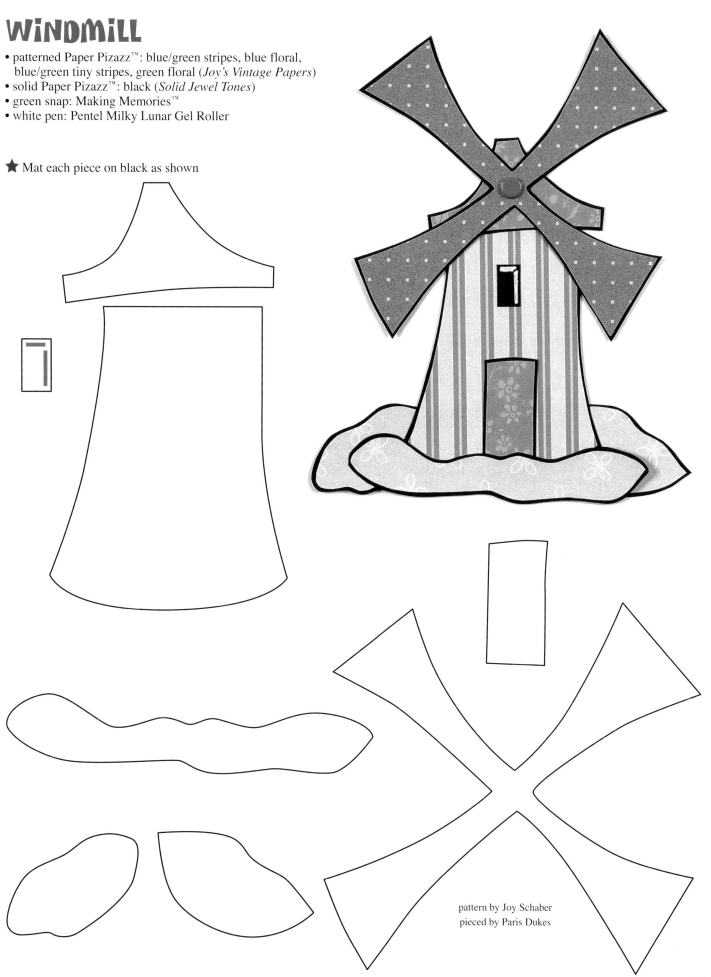

pattern by Joy Schaber
pieced by Paris Dukes

WOMAN WITH CAMERA

- patterned Paper Pizazz™: purple with daisies, purple sponged (*Mixing Light Papers*), tan webbing, tan speckled (*Soft & Subtle Textures*)
- specialty Paper Pizazz™: metallic silver* (*Metallic Silver*)
- solid Paper Pizazz™: light salmon (*Plain Pastels*), black (*Solid Jewel Tones*)
- purple fibers, buttons: Magic Scraps™
- black pen: Zebra Jimnie Gel Rollerball

★ Mat each piece on black as shown
✳ This paper is available by the sheet

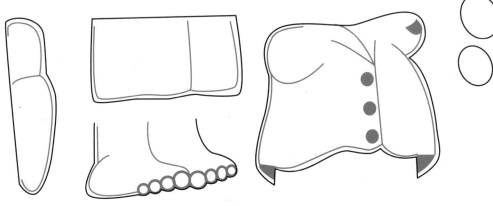

pattern by Annie Lang
pieced by Paris Dukes

ZEBRA

- patterned Paper Pizazz™: red with pink & black X's (*Mixing Heritage Papers*)
- solid Paper Pizazz™: black (*Solid Jewel Tones*)
- black fibers: Adornaments™
- white pen: Pentel Milky Lunar Gel Rollerball
- black pen: Zebra Jimnie Gel Rollerball
- adhesive foam tape: Therm O Web

★ Mat head and body on black as shown

pattern by Joy Schaber
pieced by Paris Dukes